With Friends
Like These...

With Friends Like These...

Why Britain should leave the EU
– and how

David Conway

CIVITAS
INSTITUTE FOR THE STUDY
OF CIVIL SOCIETY · LONDON

First Published August 2014

© Civitas 2014
55 Tufton Street
London SW1P 3QL

email: books@civitas.org.uk

ISBN 978-1-906837-63-1

Independence: Civitas: Institute for the Study of Civil Society is a
registered educational charity (No. 1085494) and a company limited
by guarantee (No. 04023541). Civitas is financed from a variety of
private sources to avoid over-reliance on any single or small group of
donors.

All publications are independently refereed. All the Institute's
publications seek to further its objective of promoting the
advancement of learning. The views expressed are those of the
authors, not of the Institute.

Designed and typeset by
Richard Kelly

Printed in Great Britain by
Berforts Group Ltd
Stevenage, SG1 2BH

I have always found the word 'Europe' in the mouths of those politicians who wanted from other powers something they did not dare to demand in their own name.

Otto von Bismarck

We are with Europe, but not of it, we are linked but not compromised. We are interested and associated but not absorbed.

Winston Churchill

The question I want to pose is: which picture of Europe will voters be presented with? The candid version or the cartoon version? The myths or the facts?... It's an important difference.

José Manuel Durao Barroso

Treaties are like roses and young girls – they last as long as they last.

Charles de Gaulle

England! the time is come when thou should'st wean
Thy heart from its emasculating food;
The truth should now be better understood;
Old things have been unsettled...

William Wordsworth

Contents

Author

David Conway taught philosophy for over thirty years at Middlesex University where he was head of the School of Philosophy and Religious Studies. He subsequently joined Civitas as a Senior Research Fellow and continues the association as a Visiting Professorial Research Fellow.

His publications include: *A Farewell to Marx, Classical Liberalism, The Rediscovery of Wisdom, In Defence of the Realm, A Nation of Immigrants?, Disunited Kingdom,* and *Liberal Education and the National Curriculum.*

He voted against British membership of the EEC in the 1975 Referendum, having been persuaded by the argument that the attendant loss of sovereignty would be too high a price to pay, whatever economic benefits it promised.

Acknowledgements

I should like to thank David Green for inviting me to write a monograph on this topic for Civitas, as well as Nicholas Cowen, Jonathan Lindsell, Peter Saunders and Anthony Scholefield for their many immensely helpful suggestions about how to improve on an earlier draft. If I have not always acted on their suggestions and comments, I have always very much appreciated receiving them. Any residual errors or other shortcomings are entirely my own responsibility.

Introduction

As austerity continues to ravage many parts of the European Union (EU), of one commodity there has been no shortage. That commodity is opinion as to whether a country benefits or loses out by belonging to this enigmatic, supranational organisation. The EU is indeed a perennial work-in-progress whose only point of constancy appears to be its overarching ambition to forge ever closer union between the peoples of Europe.

Unsurprisingly, the economic crisis within the eurozone has seen a remarkable collapse of trust in the EU on the part of these same peoples. According to Eurobarometer, the polling agency which for decades has conducted public opinion polls within the EU on behalf of the European Commission: 'Since the beginning of the crisis, trust in the EU has fallen from +10 to −22 points in France, from +20 to −29 points in Germany, from +30 to −22 points in Italy, from +42 to −52 in Spain, from +50 to +6 points in Poland, and from −13 to −49 points in the UK.'[1]

These figures also show that, when it comes to euroscepticism, the United Kingdom has been both pioneer and market-leader. Initially reluctant to join, and always half-hearted in its membership, the UK has long been something of an outlier in Europe. This partly reflects its geographic location. Perched on the continent's westerly rim, it is the closest, both in distance and culture, to its former colony and closest ally on the far side of the Atlantic: the United States of America.

However disenchanted with the EU the euro-crisis has

rendered continental Europe, in Britain its chief effect has been for its media to begin to accord much greater coverage to eurosceptic opinion. Until recently, public expression of such scepticism had been banished to the margins of political life, since all three major parties had for some time become officially wedded to Britain's membership of the EU. As the euro-crisis has dragged on, however, this eurosceptic strand of opinion has begun to enter into the mainstream of British politics. There are now signs that the fragile truce between leading lights of the Conservative Party over the merits of Britain's membership of the EU is starting to break down.

As the debate in Britain intensifies, more and more senior statesmen and other leading opinion-formers, both there and elsewhere, have begun to proffer opinions on the subject. One trigger of what lately has turned into a veritable cacophony of voices on the matter was a much heralded speech made by Prime Minister David Cameron in January 2013 in which he announced that, should his party gain office at the next general election, it would seek to repatriate powers from Brussels before putting the renegotiated terms of Britain's EU membership to the electorate in an in-out referendum in 2017.[2]

Whatever might have been the Prime Minister's ultimate intention in making that announcement, it had little apparent effect in stemming what has become a major haemorrhaging of electoral support for his party in favour of the United Kingdom Independence Party (UKIP) which advocates Britain's complete withdrawal from the EU. UKIP gained approximately 23 per cent of the vote in the local elections of May 2013, bringing its electoral support to a level comparable with that of Labour's 29 per cent and the Conservatives' 24 per cent.[3] That election result sent a dramatic warning to the Conservative Party, since UKIP had largely, but not exclusively, taken votes from former Conservative supporters. The shift in support towards UKIP was replicated in both the local elections and European Parliament elections of May 2014, in which it gained over 160 seats in the former elections and topped the poll in the latter one with 27.5 per cent of the vote. Even if, in the 2015 general election, UKIP's share of the vote is nothing like as big as in the 2013 and 2014 elections and not one single candidate from that party is returned to Westminster, on present showing it might still win enough votes to deny the Conservatives electoral victory.

Meanwhile, many senior Conservatives have begun to break ranks with their party's official line, which is in favour of Britain's continued membership of the EU. Instead, some have begun to signal their preference for Britain to withdraw, at least on its current terms of membership. Such figures include Education Secretary Michael Gove,[4] Defence Secretary Phillip Hammond,[5] former Defence Secretary Liam Fox,[6] Environment Secretary Owen Paterson[7] and Mayor of London Boris Johnson.[8]

The public profession of so 'heretical' an opinion by so many senior members of the Conservative Party has triggered a predictable riposte from their more europhile counterparts. Among the most notable is the Minister without Portfolio Kenneth Clarke, who has often claimed that it would be folly for Britain to leave the EU, or even to suggest that it might, because even that suggestion is liable to discourage foreign inward investment.[9]

David Cameron's speech has likewise evoked strong expressions of support for Britain's continued EU membership from many senior foreign political leaders. American President Barack Obama declared: 'The United States values a strong UK in a strong European Union, which makes critical contributions to peace, prosperity, and security in Europe and around the world.'[10] German Chancellor Angela Merkel stated: 'It's my firm conviction that we belong together, the UK and the other European member states.'[11] French President François Hollande said: 'I hope Britain stays in the European Union.'[12]

Among the first senior member of the Conservative party to break ranks with its official line on Europe and to advocate UK withdrawal was Lord (Nigel) Lawson, Chancellor of the Exchequer in Margaret Thatcher's Conservative administration between 1983 and 1989. In a lengthy opinion piece published by the *Times* on 7 May 2013, he set out why, in any future referendum on the issue, he would vote for Britain to leave:

> The heart of the matter is that the very nature of the European Union, and of this country's relationship with it, has fundamentally changed after the coming into being of the European monetary union and the creation of the eurozone of which – quite rightly – we are not a part. That is why... I shall be voting 'out' in 2017... Not only do our interests increasingly differ from those of the eurozone members but... we are now becoming increasingly marginalised as we are doomed to being consistently outvoted by the eurozone bloc... But there are other, and more important, gains than this... [T]he EU has become a bureaucratic monstrosity. This imposes substantial economic costs on all member states, perhaps greatest in the case of the UK... London remains a far more important financial centre than the rest of Europe put together... with substantial growth prospects, where the country is indisputably a world-class player... However, after the recent banking meltdown, the EU is currently engaged in a frenzy of regulatory activism... [i]n part... motivated by a jealous desire to cut London down to size, in part by well-intentioned ignorance.[13]

Two days after the publication of Lord Lawson's sentiments about the EU, they were resoundingly echoed by Michael Portillo, a fellow minister in Margaret Thatcher's government as well as one in John Major's successor administration. Arguing in support of the UK's withdrawal from the EU, rather than for any attempt to renegotiate terms, Portillo remarked of the present Conservative leadership's attitude towards EU membership (which he claimed was shared by the leadership of the other two main parties):

> [T]he senior leadership... cannot contemplate withdrawal... The default position of the [entire] political class is... that Britain could not survive outside the union and... that the public shares its defeatism... If... the British electorate [is cowed] ... into voting for continued EU membership... [it] would deliver Britain into the Euro. So the referendum, were it to occur, would... really be about pulling out or in due course entering political union...That is why I would vote 'no' and fervently hope that the British have more guts than those who govern us... The Euro is a disaster. It has created hardship, unemployment and division on a dangerous scale... The UK is unhappy in the EU. We do not share its vision... It is disingenuous to suggest that this fundamental mismatch can be resolved by a little renegotiation. [14]

The following day brought forth a rejoinder to Lord Lawson from another former Cabinet colleague in Margaret Thatcher's administration, Lord (Michael) Heseltine. It was his strong opposition to her steadily mounting antipathy towards the EU that led him to mount a challenge to her leadership which eventually brought her premiership to an end. In a comment piece in the *Financial Times*, Lord Heseltine remarked:

> In the 1980s, Margaret Thatcher sent Arthur Cockfield to Brussels... to negotiate for the UK's interest. He did it

well, opening up the continent to more of our goods and services. What nobody noticed was that, to give effect to the 1986 Single European Act, we would need to put 400 regulations through parliament... [W]e were right to take part. Had we walked away, France and Germany would have carved up the agenda... Indeed, the alternative to EU membership... is not independence. It is being told by the EU what conditions it will accept for us to trade in the European marketplace... EU membership also attracts investment into the UK... But only if our EU membership is not in doubt... Britain would not only lose out economically from leaving the union. We would also suffer geopolitically... Every Tory prime minister since Harold Macmillan... has realised that the choice is between EU membership and irrelevance... The US has been spelling this out since the end of the Second World War: what use to them is a Britain that cannot lead on its own continent? ... Influence in Europe, not isolation from it, is what Britain needs if it is to thrive.[15]

As if on cue, the Obama administration then promptly let it be known how diminished in influence Britain would become, especially in Washington, should it decide to leave the EU. According to a report by the *Guardian*'s diplomatic editor that appeared there towards the end of May: 'The Obama administration has warned British officials that if the UK leaves Europe it will exclude itself from a US-EU trade and investment partnership potentially worth hundreds of billions of pounds a year, and that it was very unlikely that Washington would make a separate deal with Britain... American officials made it clear that it would take a monumental effort to get TTIP [the Transatlantic Trade and Investment Partnership] through a suspicious Congress and that "there would be very little appetite" in Washington to do it all again with the UK if Britain walked out of Europe.'[16]

For supporters of Britain's continued EU membership that warning from Washington was a fortuitous coincidence. Or was its timing more than mere coincidence? If so, it would not be for the first time that the United States has sought in semi-covert fashion to steer Britain towards closer integration with the rest of Europe. In reality, the so-called warning was a veiled threat intended to frighten Britain into remaining where, out of concern for its own perceived national interest, the USA has always wanted Britain to be ever since the end of World War II.

At a joint press conference with the British Prime Minister in Washington in mid-May, the American President was at pains to portray his stated preference for Britain to remain an EU member as being no more than just that. He acknowledged the decision had to be that of the British people's alone. He said:

> With respect to the relationship between the UK and the EU, we have a special relationship with the United Kingdom. And we believe that our capacity to partner with a United Kingdom that is... engaged with the world is hugely important to our own interests... And I think the UK's participation in the EU is an expression of its influence and role in the world. Now, ultimately, the people of the UK have to make the decision for themselves. I will say this – that David [Cameron]'s basic point that you probably want to see if you can fix what's broken in a very important relationship before you break it off makes some sense to me... Again, I want to emphasise these are issues for the people of the United Kingdom to make a decision about, not ours.[17]

The subsequent warning issued by unnamed US officials, however, about how much Britain stood to lose by withdrawing from the EU came across more as a veiled threat than a prediction. America has its own perceived strategic reasons for wanting Britain to remain in the European Union. It believes, and not without some good reason, that by doing so the EU is likely to be more Atlanticist in outlook than it otherwise would be. Yet however close Britain and America may be, their respective national interests have not always coincided. Nor has Britain's interest always been best served by its doing whatever America has wanted it to. The US would undoubtedly have welcomed Britain's military support in Vietnam in the 1960s. It was probably best for Britain that it chose to abstain from participating in that conflict. More importantly, America does not always judge rightly where its own national interest resides when it comes to foreign policy. Al Qaeda might never have come into existence, and hence there might never have been a 9/11 with all the attendant global violence which resulted from it, had America not so enthusiastically cultivated the Taliban in their struggle against the Soviet invasion of Afghanistan in the 1980s.[18]

A propos of America's wish for Britain to remain within the EU, there is a danger that, should Britain continue down the road towards ever closer integration with its other members, in time its 'special relation' with America would become so attenuated that Britain might cease to have the ability or possibly even the will to influence European foreign policy in a direction friendly to American interests. To see how this might come about, it is worth recalling what West German Chancellor Konrad Adenauer reportedly told the French Prime Minister Guy Mollet at the height of the Suez crisis, after American opposition to the joint incursion of France and Britain into Suez had forced them to abandon their military operation: 'France and England will never be powers comparable to the United States and the Soviet Union. Nor Germany either. There remains only one way of playing a decisive role on the world; that is to unite to make Europe. England is not ripe for it but the affair of Suez will help to prepare her spirits for it... Europe will be your revenge.'[19]

A stray remark made half a century ago by a German Chancellor might be thought too remote in time and inconsequential in substance to have any contemporary relevance. Yet the attitudes that France and Germany have subsequently displayed towards participating in recent military conflicts involving the USA do not suggest anything like so great a readiness on their part to support the US militarily as Britain has tended to display. Among European nations, only Britain stood by America during the Second Gulf War of 2003. Likewise, in a UN Security Council vote in 2011, Germany alone among Western allies abstained from supporting military action against Colonel Gaddafi's regime in Libya.

In an interview with Gerhard Schröder published in *Der Spiegel* in early April 2013, the former German Chancellor concurred with his interviewer that his refusal when Chancellor to support the American invasion of Iraq in 2003 'was the point at which German foreign policy came of age'.[20] Schröder concluded the interview by observing that: 'Because of its economic power and its political significance, Germany is currently destined to assume leadership within the European Union.'

America's gambit to keep its oldest and most dependable ally within the European Union might merely result in time in its being lost *to* Europe, rather than its serving as a Trojan horse for America. Despite disclaimers by Chancellor Merkel, who has expressed doubts about the likelihood of its creation in the foreseeable future, her former foreign minister Guido Westerwelle has led a campaign for the creation of a European army among the EU's largest member states with the notable exception of Britain. In September 2012, a group of eleven EU foreign ministers spearheaded by Westerwelle published a report on the 'Future of Europe' which called for further integration and centralisation of EU foreign policy under the so-called High Representative/Vice-President of the Commission and with more decision-making by qualified majority voting. The report declared: 'To make the EU into a real actor on the global scene we believe that we should in the long term: introduce more majority decisions in the common foreign and security policy sphere, or at least prevent one single member state from being able to obstruct initiatives; seek, where possible, joint representation in international organisations; aim for a European Defence Policy with joint efforts regarding the defence industry; for some members of the group this could eventually involve a European army.'[21] If, under such future circumstances as these, America hopes Britain would be able to exert sufficient influence over European foreign and defence policy to ensure that it remains in accord with US strategic interests, then America is surely hoping in vain. It is fairly clear that it is the intention of these foreign ministers, through use of qualified majority voting, to construct a Europe free of British influence over foreign and defence policy irrespective of its membership status.

President Obama, however, is by no means the only foreign leader to have voiced strong support for Britain remaining in the EU and to hint of reprisals should it decide to leave. Addressing an assembly of British bankers in London's Guildhall a month after David Cameron's landmark speech, Herman Van Rompuy, President of the EU's Council of Ministers, said: 'Leaving the club altogether... is legally possible... But it's not a matter of just walking out. It would be legally and politically a most complicated and unpractical affair... Leaving... doesn't come for free...The wish to redefine your country's relationship with the Union has not gone unnoticed... I cannot speak on behalf of the other presidents and prime ministers, but I presume they neither particularly like it, nor particularly fear it.'[22]

Meanwhile, hardly a day has gone by since David Cameron's January 2013 speech without some fresh directive or policy announcement issuing from Brussels that has major implications for Britain. This steady flow of EU law and policy has served to perpetuate the controversy over the merits of Britain's continued EU membership.

The controversy over Britain's continued membership of the EU will undoubtedly be further exacerbated by the decision of the European Council in June 2014 to nominate Jean-Claude Juncker as President of the European Commission following the May 2014 European Parliament elections. Despite David Cameron's vociferous objections both to the nomination and to the public rationale given for it, only Hungary's prime minister joined him in opposing Juncker's nomination in the vote Cameron forced the Council to take.

The scale of Cameron's defeat reveals the width of the gulf separating Britain from the rest of Europe over the question of the future direction of the EU. Britain's prime minister is keen to reverse the level of integration already achieved, while the rest of the EU seems keen on accelerating the pace. It also suggests that David Cameron's intended renegotiation of Britain's membership terms stands little chance of success save within the context of wider intergovernmental discussions on a new EU treaty that will finally allow these two estranged parties to go their separate ways.

Like Angela Merkel, who did so much to ensure that Juncker's candidacy for EC President prevailed over Cameron's opposition, the former Luxembourg prime minister has in recent times hinted that he too would be willing to support some such new treaty.

Much overlooked in Britain at the time of the European Parliament election was the fact that, in March 2014, Juncker had been officially adopted by the EPP grouping of European political parties as their preferred candidate for EC President. It was precisely because this grouping then gained the largest share of the vote in the May elections that Juncker was able to claim that he had received an electoral mandate from the peoples of Europe as the European Parliament's so-called *Spitzenkandidat* or lead-candidate.

However dubious the logic of this argument might be, there was something else of far greater importance that was widely overlooked in Britain at the time of the May elections. This was that, as the EPP's candidate for the Presidency, Juncker had, in April 2014, set out in that group's election manifesto the priorities he would set himself if he were appointed Commission President. Among these priorities was that of 'giving an answer to the British question':

No reasonable politician can ignore the fact that, during the next five years, we will have to find solutions for the political concerns of the United Kingdom. We have to do this if we want to keep the UK within the European Union – which I would like to do as Commission President. As Commission President, I will work for a fair deal with Britain. A deal that accepts the specificities of the UK in the EU, while allowing the eurozone to integrate further. The UK will need to understand that, in the eurozone, we need more Europe, not less. On the other hand, the other EU countries will have to accept that the UK will never participate in the euro, even if we may regret this. We have to accept that the UK will not become a member of the Schengen area. And I am also ready to accept that the UK will stay outside new EU institutions such as the European Public Prosecutor's

Office, meant to improve the fight against fraud in the EU, but clearly rejected by the House of Commons and the House of Lords. We have to respect such clear positions of the British Parliament, based on the British 'opt out' protocol. David Cameron has recently written down a number of further key demands... As Commission President, I will be ready to talk to him about these demands in a fair and reasonable manner. My red line in such talks would be the integrity of the single market and its four freedoms; and the possibility to have more Europe within the eurozone to strengthen the single currency shared so far by 18 and soon by 19 member states. But I have the impression that this is as important for Britain as it will be for the next President of the Commission. A deal that accepts the specificities of the UK in the EU.[23]

The more Europe for eurozone countries, of which Juncker here declares himself to be in favour, could well require a new EU treaty. This would give Britain the opportunity to regain for itself the powers that Cameron has declared that he wishes Britain to repatriate from Brussels. Juncker will not have been oblivious to this fact. So there could well be much about which the British electorate will have cause to ponder, come the promised in/out referendum on British membership of the EU in 2017.

Come an eventual in-out referendum, how the poor benighted British public is expected to be able to take account of all the supposedly relevant considerations before deciding how to vote is well worth pondering over. Doubtless, beforehand, a protracted debate will have taken place within the British media, as happened soon after Britain entered the EEC, when in a referendum in 1975 its electorate was invited to register support or opposition for its membership. As we shall presently see, however, what transpired on that past occasion hardly provides cause for optimism that any future referendum will be the product of a truly informed decision.

Consider, for example, the advice the British diplomat who was *chef de cabinet* to one of Britain's two EEC Commissioners recalls having given them on how best they should set about renegotiating Britain's terms of membership. The advice was contained in a report circulated among all the EEC Commissioners: 'The British will call all sorts of things "renegotiations" which we [the Commission] know aren't renegotiation. Just don't contradict them, let them get on with it, because anything they choose to score as renegotiation which is achieved in the normal run of transacting European business – that's fine -- why get into an argument about whether it's got this label "renegotiation"?'[24]

The 1975 referendum was seriously compromised by both a considerable degree of deliberate misinformation, as well as covert funding from foreign vested interests. Together, they have left a question-mark over the legitimacy of its result all these decades later. What transpired in the run-up to that earlier referendum on Europe, therefore, should serve Britain as a timely warning as to the profound limitations of all such exercises in public opinion-forming and decision-making.

As calls in Britain grow ever more insistent for an in/ out referendum on its membership of the EU and as the odds of it happening shorten, it is worth considering how and why the EU came into being and Britain joined as a prelude to considering whether Britain has gained or lost through having done so. Should Britain be judged to have lost out through its EU membership, the question then arises of how best it might set about extricating itself from the EU and what future relationship with it Britain should seek to establish instead. The historical matters will be considered in chapter one. Chapter two will examine the alleged economic benefits and true costs of Britain's EU membership. Chapter three will examine the political costs and benefits of membership. The overall verdict will be that Britain has indeed lost out both economically and politically by being a member. Accordingly, the fourth and final chapter will consider how best Britain might set about leaving the EU and what alternative relationship it should seek to forge with it.

1

The European Union: its Origins and Rationale

Received wisdom *vs* inconvenient truth

According to the received narrative, the EU project began when France and Germany agreed, shortly after the end of World War II, to place their coal and steel industries under a new supranational authority.[1] The resources and plants they wished above all to see placed under joint authority were for the most part situated in their mutual borderline region of Alsace-Lorraine and the Saar. During the previous century, both regions had changed hands between them several times, on each occasion after bloody conflict. By placing their coal and iron deposits under a joint supranational authority, France and Germany sought to eliminate a possible cause of future wars, as well as to facilitate their post-war economic reconstruction.

Other European countries were invited to join the project which led, in 1952, to the creation of the European Coal and Steel Community (ECSC). This was the nucleus and model for the further critical step towards European integration taken five years later in Rome. Then, France, Germany and Italy, plus the three Benelux countries, signed a further pair of treaties. One of these two 1957 Rome treaties established the European Atomic Energy Community. The other established the European Economic Community (EEC), better known at the time in Britain as the Common Market. While welcoming and supporting the bodies that these treaties created, Britain declined invitations to join all three of them.

The idea that the countries of Europe should unite economically and politically in the interests of peace preceded the end of World War II. According to the accepted version of the emergence of the EU,[2] the idea of a European union first arose Phoenix-like out of the ashes marking the end of World War I. Enthusiasm for the project was temporarily put on hold in the 1930s and 1940s by the rise of Nazism and Fascism and the resultant world-wide conflagration to which they led. The idea, however, was reputedly reborn within various groups of Resistance fighters during the Second World War who, upon cessation of hostilities in 1945 were finally able to turn their vision into a reality.

The view that the European Union enjoys impeccably liberal credentials has now become entrenched. However, it offers only a very one-sided and partial account of the historical record. Airbrushed from the record are four highly inconvenient facts for those intent upon portraying the EU as an essentially benign and liberal organisation.

First, anti-fascist resistance fighters were by no means the only protagonists in World War II to resurrect the idea of uniting Europe as an antidote to future war: the idea had been just as enthusiastically embraced by the Nazis. Second, European Union was not first conceived during the inter-war years; its provenance is much older, with roots going back at least as far as to the writings of the mid-nineteenth century German economist Friedrich List. His proposals for a European union were later to be adopted not just by the Nazis, but, before that, by the late nineteenth-century movement known as Pan-Germanism, the source of the aggressive nationalism marking German foreign policy during the first half of the twentieth century. Third, much of the funding behind the organisations created after the end of World

War II to promote the cause of European union came from the USA whose main concern in financing them was not to prevent future war between its member states. It was rather to prevent the continent from falling under communist rule. Fourth, covert CIA funding and other forms of covert action were pivotal in shifting public opinion in Britain from original hostility towards the idea of joining a European union into subsequent support. The CIA involvement lasted right up to the 1975 referendum on British membership of the EEC and undoubtedly helped determine its outcome of a majority vote in favour of British membership.

These four inconvenient truths put an entirely different complexion upon how genuinely benign an organisation the European Union is, as well as upon what reason Britain has, or ever has had, to be a part of it. Each will now be taken up in turn.

Pan-Germanism as prime mover of European integration

In his contribution to the compendious anthology *Documents on the History of European Integration: Volume 1 Continental Plans for European Union 1939–45*, the German military historian Michael Salewski observed that: 'From the outset of the war it was a staple of Nazi propaganda that the Reich was waging the struggle "imposed" on it for the sake of a "new Europe".'[3] A couple of quotations from the anthology illustrate just how central a role the ideal of European union played in Nazi rhetoric and thinking at the time.

In May 1940, Arthur Seyss-Inquart, a leading Austrian National Socialist, was appointed Reich Commissioner of the occupied Netherlands. Shortly afterwards, the new Reich Commissioner was to declare that: 'The European area is combining to form a new order... a new Europe is being formed, strong by reason of its size and the coordination of its needs...'[4] A short while later, he added:

> Above and beyond the concept of a nation state, the
> idea of a new community will transform the living space
> given us all by history into a new spiritual realm... The
> new Europe of solidarity and cooperation... will find an
> assured foundation and rapidly increasing prosperity
> once national economic barriers are removed. It will no
> longer offer to its adversaries a temptation to violate its
> peace by wars and economic wars... Nations and human
> beings only develop to the full when they participate in
> a great common destiny.[5]

In 1942, Walter Funk, the Reich's Economic Minister
and President of the Reichsbank, stated in a contribution
to an anthology published that year in Berlin under the
title of *The European Economic Community*:

> The English moral philosophy of Hobbes and Hume ...
> tinged with a shot of Jewish spirit from David Ricardo has
> proved to be an extraordinarily safe and imperceptibly
> effective means for justifying and safeguarding British
> world superiority... But th[e] type of freedom [they
> extolled] was of too poor moral foundation to have been
> of any real substance... Europe's peoples... all know
> now... that the freedom ideal of the past era was false
> and perishable... By creating a European economic bloc,
> we want to protect ourselves from this system... The will
> to achieve European cooperation...is the ultimate goal
> that we demand of the European nations and that we
> strive for... From the noblest blood spilt, a better social
> order for life in Europe will and must grow.[6]

That the Nazis were aiming to unite Europe under
German hegemony was known early on during the War.
As early as March 1940, the British journalist Dorothy

Thompson reported in her regular column in the *New York Herald Tribune*:

> The Germans have a clear plan of what they intend to do in case of victory... I have heard it from a sufficient number of important Germans and persons closely in touch with important Germans to credit its authenticity... Germany's plan is to make a customs union of Europe, with complete financial and economic control centred in Berlin. This will create at once the largest free trade area... in the world... The Germans count upon political power following economic power, and not vice versa. Territorial changes do not concern them, because there will be no 'France' or 'England' except as language groups... As far as the United States is concerned, the planners of World Germanica... say that it will be... force[d] to play ball... France will be kept to agriculture and the manufacture of quality goods... London is to cease to be a financial centre, but will be the chief commercial centre, under Nazi domination.[7]

So much for the notion that, during the Second World War, the idea of European Union was championed only by those fighting *against* the Nazis and Fascists. While this notion prevails within Europhile circles, it is untrue to the historical record, as recently made clear by German journalist Rainer Hank, senior economics and finance editor of the *Frankfurter Allgemeine Zeitung*. In an article first published in German in November 2013, Hank writes:

> While the German right wing was anti-European after 1918, there was a veritable 'craze for Europe' (Ulrich Herbert) after the victory over France in 1940... Adolf Hitler himself was not noted for his commitment to the 'European ideal' but, according to Goebbels' diaries, on 8 May 1943, Hitler uttered the following: 'It must remain

our war aim to create a united Europe. But Europe can only undergo clear organisation through Germany.' The point here is that the 'invention of Europe' is not – contrary to what official documents from the Council of the European Union would have us believe – a monopoly of the anti-fascist resistance.[8]

In his 1997 history of the EU, economic historian Martin Dedman asserts that: 'Movements to unite Europe politically only emerged post-World War 1.'[9] However, such movements had already begun in the late-nineteenth century with the advent of the German political movement known as Pan-Germanism of which Nazism was but a twentieth century flowering, as was recognised by the Austrian economist Ludwig von Mises in his 1944 book *Omnipotent Government: The Rise of the Total State and Total War* who observes there:

> The essential ideas of Nazism were developed by the Pan-Germans and the socialists of the chair in the last thirty years of the nineteenth century. The system was completed long before the outbreak of the First World War. Nothing was lacking and nothing but a new name was added later. The plans and policies of the Nazis differ from those of their predecessors in imperial Germany only in the fact that they are adapted to a different constellation of political conditions. The ultimate aim, German world hegemony, and the means for its attainment, have not changed.[10]

Pan-Germanism was the subject of a book published in 1915 by Charles Andler, a French professor of German language and literature at the University of Paris. In this book, several late nineteenth-century pan-German authors are quoted one of whom was Julius von Eckardt, historian, diplomat and secretary of the German Senate under Bismarck. From an 1892 book by Eckardt entitled, *Berlin-Vienna-Rome: Reflections on the new course and the new situation in Europe*, Andler quotes the following passage which he prefaces by the heading '*Germany wishes to found a Customs Union as well as a Military Union of the Central European States*', a statement which Andler claims 'exactly expresses' Eckardt's thought.[11] The quotation runs:

> The establishment... of an alliance at once political and economic between the three Central European Powers might *become the starting-point of a new European system...* A great Customs Union, created on the initiative of Germany, would prove to the world irrefutably that the foundation of the German Empire had been a necessity and a benefit for Europe... [I]t could no longer be cast in our teeth that the great German undertaking of 1870 had resulted merely in universal armaments, universal military service, and an elaboration of militarism, which is sucking out the marrow of the bones of all nations.[12]

Pan-Germanism was no mere abstract intellectual creed. It was rather a political movement, manifested by the founding in 1894 of the Pan-German League. Until 1908, the League was led by Ernst Hasse, a professor of statistics at the University of Leipzig, who, between 1893 and 1903, was also a representative in the Reichstag of the National Liberal Party. Between 1905 and 1907, Hasse published a three-volume work entitled *German Politics* from which Andler quotes the following passage:

> The future territory of German expansion, situated between the territories of the Eastern and Western powers, must absorb all the intermediate regions; it must stretch from the North Sea and the Baltic through the Netherlands, taking in Luxembourg and Switzerland, down to the lands of the Danube and the Balkan

peninsula. All foreign influence must be eliminated from this great territory... We want territory, and not merely colonies. We want territory, even if it be inhabited by foreign peoples, so that we may shape their future in accordance with our needs.[13]

Andler concludes his account of Pan-Germanism by reproducing the order of the day that Kaiser Wilhelm II issued German troops in June 1915, and which was found subsequently in the possession of captured German soldiers. The Kaiser's ominous words run: 'The triumph of Great Germany, destined one day to dominate all Europe, is the sole object of the struggle in which we are engaged.'[14]

A major source of inspiration for Pan-Germanism was the nineteenth-century German economist Friedrich List. List favoured European union, not to prevent war between European states, but rather to enable mainland European countries to wage economic war more effectively against their more industrially advanced neighbour across the English Channel. In his 1844 tract *National System of Political Economy*, List declared:

If... Germany could constitute itself with... Holland, Belgium, and Switzerland, as a powerful commercial and political whole... Germany could secure peace to the continent of Europe for a long time, and at the same time constitute herself the central point of a durable Continental alliance... If we only consider the enormous interests which the nations of the Continent have in common, as opposed to the English maritime supremacy, we shall be led to the conviction that nothing is so necessary to these nations as union.[15]

List forecast that, following the chastening experience of seeing itself overtaken economically by a united continent, Britain would seek and gain admission to a European union, in part so as to insulate herself against what he further predicted would be the still greater economic might of the Unites States of America:

> Great Britain will be compelled to seek and to find in the leadership of the united powers of Europe protection, security, and compensation against the predominance of America, and an equivalent for her lost supremacy. It is therefore good for England that she should... gain the friendship of European Continental power... [and] accustom herself betimes to the idea of being only the first among equals.[16]

The historian Paul Winkler had little difficulty in perceiving the roots of Nazism to lie in Pan-Germanism and in the writings of Friedrich List. His 1943 book *The Thousand-Year Conspiracy: Secret Germany Behind the Mask* observes:

> *Mein Kampf...* and its author, Hitler, are not the source of all evil in present-day Germany... In the ideas of List, we find... the complete outline of Germany's recent and present economic attitude... Hitler is merely applying the century-old thesis of List in the economic sphere.[17]

According to received accounts of its early history, the two chief architects of the European Union were the Frenchmen Jean Monnet and Robert Schuman. Both were serving in the post-war administration of Charles de Gaulle, Monnet as Planning Commissioner concerned with their country's post-war economic reconstruction and Schuman as Foreign Minister. At that time, old rivalries between France and Germany were beginning to resurface over the industrially rich Saar border region. To end once and for all any possibility of further armed conflict between them, the received account of the EU's history has it that Monnet contrived the idea that the two countries should pool sovereignty over their respective mineral wealth and heavy industry. Monnet put this idea to Schuman who, receiving it favourably, then publicly proposed it on 9 May 1950 in the famous declaration bearing his name but which, in reality, had been drafted almost entirely by Monnet with the assistance of a young French law professor from whom Monnet had sought technical advice. The core of the so-called Schuman Declaration runs thus:

> It is no longer a question of vain words but of a bold act, a constructive act. France has acted and the consequences of its action can be immense... France has acted primarily for peace and to give peace a real chance. For this it is necessary that Europe should exist. Five years, almost to the day, after the unconditional surrender of Germany, France is accomplishing the first decisive act for European construction and is associating Germany with this... Europe will be born from this, a Europe which is solidly united and constructed around a strong framework... The gathering of the nations of Europe demands the elimination of the age-old antagonism of France and Germany...

> With this objective in mind, the French government proposes to direct its action on one limited but decisive point: *The French government proposes to place Franco-German production of coal and steel under one common High Authority in an organisation open to the participation of other countries of Europe... By pooling basic industrial production and setting-up a new High Authority whose decisions will be binding on France, Germany and other member countries, these proposals will bring to reality the first solid groundwork for European Federation vital to the preservation of world peace.*[18]

According to the received account, the proposals contained in the Schuman Declaration won immediate acceptance from West Germany's Chancellor Konrad Adenauer. The three Benelux countries and Italy quickly joined in the project, leading, via the Treaty of Paris of April 1951, to the creation of the European Coal and Steel Community under the presidency of Jean Monnet. The truth, however, is somewhat more complex and murkier.

In proposing the European Coal and Steel Community, Monnet had been responding to a still more radical proposal for removing possible cause of future conflict between France and Germany. This more radical proposal called for their full-scale union and it had been made by West German Chancellor Konrad Adenauer in an interview with the head of the European bureau of the International News Service in March 1950. Upon its publication, the reaction in France had largely been one of horror: 'Adenauer wants to build Europe around Germany and for Germany,' commented the French newspaper *L'Aube*.[19]

It was, therefore, as a less radical but more realistic alternative to Adenauer's proposal that Monnet had come up with his own proposal, known to posterity as the Schuman Declaration. This is something Monnet himself acknowledged in his *Memoirs*.[20]

March 1950 was, however, by no means the first time that Adenauer had publicly floated the idea of Franco-German union. As early as March 1946, three years before he became Chancellor, Adenauer had declared at a meeting of the Rhineland and Westphalia branch of the newly formed Christian Democrat Party: 'It is my deepest belief that the United States of Europe can finally bring peace to this continent which has been ravaged by war so often.'[21]

It is small wonder, then, that, when in late May 1950 Monnet duly visited Adenauer in Bonn to discuss the

Schuman Plan, at the end of their meeting the West German Chancellor had risen to his feet and declared: 'Monsieur Monnet, I regard the implementation of the French proposal as my most important task. If I succeed, I believe my life will not have been wasted.'[22]

In advocating Franco-German union, Adenauer's prime motive had been to prevent the Saarland from becoming permanently lost to Germany as France had proposed initially after the war. Adenauer managed to accomplish his objective, however, not by persuading anyone that their union was needed to prevent war between France and Germany. It was rather by convincing America that the union was needed to prevent future military conflict between itself and the Soviet Union.

At the time of its creation in 1949, West Germany was still a remarkably weak state, bordering as it did the Soviet sphere of influence on its eastern flank and having been completely disarmed. America was desperate to see West Germany strengthened in order to help meet the threat of potential invasion by the Soviet Union. By cleverly playing on American Cold War anxieties, Adenauer managed to convince America of the need for European Union.

The covert US financing of European union

Action Committee for the United States of Europe
The Action Committee for the United States of Europe was one of three organisations created in the early years of the Cold War with the help of generous covert CIA funding to promote the cause of European integration. The three organisations received funding from the CIA because, at the time, the American defence establishment viewed European integration as the best means of combating what it perceived to be a very real threat of Soviet invasion of Europe or communist subversion. The

funding was covert so as to prevent the three organisations from being regarded as agents of American imperialism. As Ambrose Evans-Pritchard reported in the *Telegraph* in September 2000:

> Declassified American government documents show that the US intelligence community ran a campaign in the fifties and sixties to build momentum for a united Europe. It funded and directed the European federalist movement... The leaders of the European Movement – [Joseph] Retinger, the visionary Robert Schuman and the former Belgian prime minister Paul-Henri Spaak – were all treated as hired hands by their American sponsors. The US role was handled as a covert operation... The State Department also played a role. A memo from the European section, dated June 11, 1965, advises the vice-president of the European Economic Community, Robert Marjolin, to pursue monetary union by stealth. It recommends suppressing debate until the point at which 'adoption of such proposals would become virtually inescapable'.[23]

The Action Committee no longer exists. Not so the other two organisations, namely, the European Movement and the Bilderberg Group.

European Movement

The European Movement was created in New York in October 1948. It was formed in the wake of the Hague Congress of Europe the previous May that had led to the establishment of the Council of Europe. Initially, the European Movement was placed under the leadership of Duncan Sandys, son-in-law of Winston Churchill, who had called for European union, but without Britain's membership of it, in a landmark speech at the University of Zurich in 1946. Initially, the CIA had been keen to fund Sandys in that role.

However, American enthusiasm for Sandys and for British leadership of the European Movement began to wane after it became apparent that Britain favoured the more strictly intergovernmental Council of Europe, based in Strasbourg, to the more radical supra-national form of European integration proposed by the likes of Monnet, Schuman and Adenauer. Since the European Movement was principally funded by the CIA, it was quickly able to arrange the transfer of its headquarters from London to Brussels, and of its leadership to the distinctly more Europhile former Belgian Prime Minister Paul-Henri Spaak, who, in 1952, became the first President of the ECSC Assembly in Strasbourg, forerunner of the European Parliament.

Bilderberg Group

The Bilderberg Group is the other still-extant organisation set up in the early 1950s with covert CIA funding to promote the cause of European integration as well as the transatlantic alliance. Unlike the two other Europeanist organisations established with CIA funding, this group does not wear its Europhilic proclivities so conspicuously on its sleeve. However, there can be little doubt that, among its aims, European integration was, and most likely still remains, a central one.

Stephen Dorril and Richard J. Aldrich are the two foremost British academic authorities on the activities of western security and intelligence services during the Cold War. Both contend that the Bilderberg Group was created with the help of CIA funding for the purpose of promoting European integration.

Concerning the circumstances surrounding its creation, Dorril supplies the following information in his 2000 study of the activities of MI6 during the second half of the twentieth century:

During 1952, Retinger suggested... the idea of organising unofficial meetings of leading personalities from NATO countries with the purpose of 'promoting European unity and an Atlantic alliance'... A meeting was held in September, in Paris, during which an advisory committee was created.[24]

[T]he first formal Bilderberg conference was held in May [1954] in the small Dutch town of Oosterbeekat, at the Hotel de Bilderberg, from which the meeting took its name. It was seen as an opportunity for shapers of opinion among elite groups in Europe to speak with one voice to their counterparts in the United States who feared that differences over European integration and eastern Europe would create misunderstandings. Funding came courtesy of the Dutch government and the CIA.[25]

In his magisterial 2001 survey of the activities of British and American intelligence services during the Cold War, Aldrich supplies the following further details about the extent of CIA involvement with the Group and its funding: 'By the early 1950s promoting European unity was the largest CIA operation in Western Europe... Quite simply, the most enthusiastic federalist power in post-war Europe was the United States.'[26]

Given what Dorril and Aldrich claim to have been the extent of American involvement in promoting European union after the War, it would appear that the public warning T.H. Tetens gave US President Dwight Eisenhower in the 1950s had fallen on deaf ears:

As a political analyst who has spent a lifetime in fighting Germany's bid for world conquest in two world wars, I see the old plot emerging again in the words and deeds of the new Germany... We have not learned our lessons from the past. Twice within a generation we went to war in order to stop German aggression. Each time we gained military victory, only to throw it away by making Germany strong again as a 'bulwark against the East'... If the Germans have their way, it will happen again.[27]

A European Union with Germany as its strongest pillar will turn out to be the greatest blunder. Germany's industry will not only dominate the markets in Europe... [A] resurrected strong Germany will see her future task in the creation of a third Power Bloc... clearly demonstrated by Dr Adenauer's speeches and articles in which he told his fellow Germans about the great advantages of the Schuman Plan.... A united Europe, he said, will 'become the Third Force in the world, powerful enough to intervene successfully – in a decisive moment – to safeguard the peace'.[28]

In December 1951, the leading West German geo-political newspaper *Christ und Welt* had expressed much the same misgivings as those of Tetens. It had warned: 'Continental Europe would break away from the Atlantic Pact... A Western Europe standing on its own feet and possessing its own powerful army... could afford to carry out such an independent policy because it will have the strength of a third power.'[29]

Germany's present-day domination of Europe

Since its reunification in 1990, Germany has not only come to assume *de facto* leadership of the European Union, it has also begun to play, as well as to call for the EU to play, a more active role on the international stage outside of NATO. Neither of these trends accords well with Britain's national interest for reasons to be given in chapter three.

As it was originally conceived, the European Union

was to be a partnership between west European countries all at approximately the same level of economic development. With the collapse of communism at the end of the 1980s, all that changed. West Germany immediately sought and achieved its unification with East Germany, at once thereby becoming the largest country within the EU by far. As the price that France demanded for allowing its unification, Germany relinquished its cherished Deutschmark for the euro. Behind France's demand was the calculation that monetary union would bind Germany so closely to its other eurozone partners as to prevent it from posing a threat to them.

As part of its price for giving up the Deutschmark, Germany demanded that European monetary union be accomplished on German terms with a Frankfurt-based European central bank and price stability as its central goal. In his 1994 account of the events of this critical period *Germany and Europe: The Crisis of Unity*, the then European Editor of the *Financial Times* David Marsh recounted how, in December 1991 at Maastricht, he was informed by Dietrich von Kyaw, then head of the German Foreign Office's directorate for European Community affairs, that: 'To counter German unease that the future European currency would be less than stable... the site for the planned European central bank should be in Frankfurt.'[30] This German objective was achieved in 1993.

Without an accompanying common banking and fiscal policy, it would only be a matter of time before the common currency led to profound economic dislocations within the eurozone. Its economically weaker members have been priced out of the international markets by a currency of which the value was beyond their control. Meanwhile, Germany has taken advantage of their economic weakness, since it has made the euro lower in value on the foreign exchange markets than it otherwise would have been, thereby making its exports cheaper on international markets. The result has been for the economically weaker member states of the eurozone to have become mired in debt to a booming Germany which, by virtue of its power over them as their major creditor, has increasingly been able to set monetary policy.

Should the present euro-crisis eventually lead members of the eurozone to agree to full-scale fiscal and banking union, as many within Europe are currently advocating, this will again be on Germany's terms. As, therefore, the eurozone slowly consolidates into a United States of Europe, EU members outside of the eurozone such as Britain will face increasing pressure either to join the common currency or else leave the EU. In sum, should Britain remain within the European Union, within a fairly short period it is likely to become subject to increased foreign governance by a union that will correspondingly have become dominated by Germany.

For many other EU member states, the prospect of their becoming absorbed within a newly emergent United States of Europe will not pose too much of a problem, especially if their only experience of independent statehood has been recent and short-lived. For Great Britain, however, to become absorbed within and subject to rule by a federal union would be felt as nothing short of a political disaster and wholly unacceptable. With extreme prescience and a customary bluntness that cost him his position as Secretary of State for Trade in Industry in the final period of Margaret Thatcher's administration, Nicholas Ridley explained exactly why in an interview published in the *Spectator*. Of the European Community, as it was called then, Ridley remarked:

This is all a German racket designed to take over the whole of Europe... the German people... already run most of the Community. I mean they pay half of the countries... The point is that when it comes to 'Shall we apply more squeeze to the economy or shall we let up a bit?' this is essentially about political accountability... [T]he British people... can be dared; they can be moved. But being bossed by a German – it would cause absolute mayhem in this country... There could be a bloody revolution.[31]

In a retrospective article about that notorious interview published in the same journal a decade later, Dominic Lawson spelt out the essential reason why there could be such a revolt. He observed: 'The issue here is sovereignty, not economics... [Ridley's] point was that those imposing harsh measures have to be elected by the people on the receiving end.'[32]

In short, what from Britain's point of view is fundamentally unacceptable about continued membership of the European Union is that it will inexorably lead to its increasingly becoming subject to rule by foreigners – specifically, by Germans.

Decades before Lawson and Ridley claimed this, Ludwig von Mises made a similar claim, putting his finger on what he contended to be the ultimate design flaw in any such form of union. In 1944, Mises wrote about the idea of a post-war union of western European democracies then being mooted:

The main obstacle to... a super-national customs union... [is that it] requires unlimited supremacy of the super-national authorities and an almost complete annihilation of the national governments... The Prime Minister of Great Britain... [would be reduced] to the status of provincial governor... and Parliament to [a] provincial assembl[y]. It is unlikely that the... British will easily agree to such a solution of their problem. It is futile to ask people whether they are in favour of a renunciation of their own nation's sovereignty. Most laymen do not understand the meaning of the term 'sovereignty'. The correct formulation for the question would be: Do you advocate a system under which your nation could be forced to submit to a measure which the majority of your fellow citizens oppose? Are you ready to see essential laws of your country (for example, immigration laws) altered by a Union Parliament in which the members returned by your country are a minority only? [33]

By way of rebuttal, it might be stated that what Mises predicted the British would never accept is precisely what they did accept at the time of the 1975 referendum, when a majority of the votes cast were in favour of Britain remaining in the EEC into which Edward Heath's Conservative administration had taken it three years earlier. However, at the time of that referendum, the British public had been very badly misled as to the kind of organisation they were being asked to commit to.

How Britain was duped into joining the EEC

At the time Britain joined the European Economic Community, it had only been possible to render the step palatable to the British public by carefully concealing from it the true nature and purpose of the supranational entity to which their country had been signed up. The act of concealment was accomplished by the EEC's having been portrayed as a mere 'common market' through entry to which Britain would lose no 'essential sovereignty' – although the entire political class must have known otherwise.

Until 1961, both main political parties in Britain had opposed joining the EEC precisely because Britain would lose sovereignty. In 1961, however, Harold Macmillan's Conservative administration changed its previous policy on the issue and decided to make a formal application for Britain to join. For several months prior to his announcing that decision to the House of Commons, there had been Cabinet discussions on the issue. At one of them, the then Lord Chancellor Lord Kilmuir had presented a paper on the impact that entry would have on the country's legal and parliamentary system. It concluded that: 'Parliament would be required to surrender some of its functions to the organs of the Community. The Crown would be called on to transfer part of its treaty-making power to those organs. Our courts of law would sacrifice some degree of independence by becoming subordinate in certain respects to the European Court of Justice.'[34]

Lord Kilmuir's concerns were never made known to the British public at the time.

Instead, later that same summer, Britain was to make its first formal application to join the EEC. Its negotiating team was led by the Lord Privy Seal Edward Heath, a consistent advocate of British participation in European integration ever since his maiden speech to the House of Commons in June 1950 in which he had vainly exhorted Atlee's Labour administration to participate in the Schuman Plan.

In the decade between Heath's maiden speech and Macmillan's announcement of his intention to apply for British membership of the EEC, much had happened to bring the Prime Minister and most of his Cabinet around to Heath's point of view. Above all, three factors account for the U-turn by the Conservative Party at the start of the 1960s.

First, there was the failure by Britain, in 1958 and again in 1960, to join the six EEC West European countries in forming a free trade area in manufactured goods. As a result of this failure, Britain became increasingly fearful of the economic consequences of being locked out of major European markets at a time when its trading links with former colonies and overseas dominions were becoming ever more attenuated.

Second, after the failure of the Suez venture in 1956, it was made increasingly apparent to Britain that it could no longer expect to enjoy its historic 'special relationship' with the USA unless it joined the EEC which would otherwise inherit it. As US Under-Secretary of State Douglas Dillon made clear to Macmillan on a visit to London in 1959: 'the US government would continue to support the EEC for political reasons whereas the EFTA was regarded as a purely economic grouping which involved considerable discrimination against the EU'.[35]

Third, neither of Britain's main political parties appeared able, or at least willing, to take the action that would have been needed to curb excessive trade union wage demands which were profoundly damaging to the international competitiveness of its manufactured goods. Both parties hoped that, as a result of joining the EEC, British workers would become subject to a form of wage discipline. As the historian A.J.P. Taylor observed in 1962, when Britain first applied to join the EEC, in words that apply equally to its two subsequent attempts to join, first unsuccessfully in 1967 and then successfully in 1972:

The Common Market is, for the Government, an end in itself, which will automatically provide a solution for all ills... [Domestic] economic policy has been a failure. Instead of prosperity and expansion, there has been stagnation... The Common Market is to provide the answer. Once we are inside, Dr. Adenauer and President de Gaulle will reveal, in a kindly way, the secret of expansion... The move into the Common Market has been, from first to last, a confession by British Ministers that they did not know what to do... Entry into the Common Market is not a policy. It is a substitute for a policy. Its consequences, its implications are never explained.[36]

Initially, after Harold Macmillan announced his intention to apply for British membership of the EEC, public opinion in Britain was favourably disposed towards the idea. It quickly cooled, however, so much so that, by September 1962, the Cabinet decided: 'public opinion was getting dangerously sceptical and needed correction'.[37]

To sway public opinion back towards favouring British entry, a government-backed campaign was mounted under the superintendence of Sir Frank Lee, a senior civil servant at the Treasury and ardent Europhile. Between February 1963 and March 1964, despite President de Gaulle's veto of Britain's previous application, public support for Britain's entry increased from 42 per cent to 57 per cent, according to Gallup Polls.

Britain's second formal application was made in May 1967 during Harold Wilson's Labour administration, only to be rebuffed again by de Gaulle the following November. In his 2000 book, *Separate Ways: The Heart of Europe*, Peter Shore, a cabinet minister at the time, recounts how, shortly after that second rebuff, John Armstrong Robinson, head of the department for European Economic Integration at the Foreign Office, deliberately chose to scupper any prospect that Britain might yet be able to strike a favourable trade deal with the EEC without joining. According to Shore, he did this by deliberately leaking details of a private conversation between the British Ambassador and de Gaulle in November 1969 in which the French President had intimated that such a deal might be possible. The leak led to a row between Paris and London that permanently put paid to the possibility. Of the leak, Shore writes: 'It was clearly deliberate... No disciplinary action was taken. Clearly [whoever had made it] ... enjoyed a close and protective relationship with top FCO officials. He was... part of a "militant vanguard", an "elite regiment" of committed Europhiles, then taking key positions in the FCO. There are reasons to fear a number of them, including those they recruited, are there still.'[38]

Shortly after this episode, de Gaulle was replaced as President of France by the more Anglophile George Pompidou, thereby reopening the prospects for Britain to enter the EEC. By this time, Harold Wilson too had been replaced as Britain's Prime Minister by ardent Europhile Ted Heath, after a Conservative victory in the 1970 general election.

In July 1971, the Conservative government published a White Paper on British entry, preparing the way for a third formal attempt at joining. Although the White Paper mentioned that food prices in Britain would rise upon its entry, it made no mention of economic and monetary union, despite the original six members of the EEC having by then become committed to it.

By the time that the White Paper was published, public support for British entry into the EEC had fallen dramatically. Between 1967 and 1971, Gallup polls recorded a decline in support from 65 to 22 per cent. Another Gallup poll in April 1970 found only 19 per cent in favour, with more than 50 per cent opposed in principle to reopening negotiations.

To bolster public support for a third application, the Heath government turned to the Information Research Department (IRD). This was a semi-secret department of the Foreign Office set up immediately after the war to produce Cold War anti-communist propaganda. Geoffrey Tucker, a former Conservative Party Publicity Officer, arranged for a series of regular weekly breakfast meetings at the Connaught Hotel to which senior BBC and ITN executives with oversight of news and current affairs programmes were invited, plus the head of the IRD as well as the top aide to Britain's negotiating minister, senior industrialists, leading government and opposition politicians, friendly journalists and representatives of the European Movement. Peter Shore explains:

> [A]t the time it was assumed that the European Movement... had met the bill. In fact... the breakfasts were paid for by the IRD itself and their contribution hidden in the accounts of the European Movement. The media breakfasts were a most important part of the total effort to shift opinion in the UK. The involvement of senior officials of the Foreign Office and senior executives of the BBC in a covert propaganda campaign was a disgraceful breach of the relevant codes of conduct affecting Crown servants and of the BBC's Charter obligations. The whole operation was a closely guarded secret. It was brought to an end, after the crucial October 1971 White Paper vote, only through the personal intervention of the Head of the civil service, Sir William Armstrong.[39]

The propaganda campaign had the desired effect. With Gallup polls showing a revival of support for British membership, the Government decided to introduce a bill in favour of entry in October 1971. The Treaty of Accession was signed in January 1972 at the same time as the government introduced its European Communities Bill, which passed into law on 1 October 1972.

The matter was not yet settled, however. A Gallop poll in January 1973 found that only 38 per cent of the British public were in favour of Britain's having entered the EEC, with 36 per cent against. In the general election campaign of February 1974, the Labour party pledged that, if returned to office, it would hold an in-out referendum after renegotiating terms.

After its electoral victory, Prime Minister Harold Wilson managed to extract some minor concessions from the EEC before putting Britain's membership to the public in the form of a referendum in June 1975. The campaign in favour of Britain's EU membership won by a large margin, 67.2 per cent of votes cast being in favour and 32.8 per cent against.

What is so striking about the 1975 referendum result is how quickly, and by how much, initial public opposition towards Britain's continued membership of the EEC became transformed into support. Between January and April 1975, there was a 22 per cent swing in favour of British membership. When Gallup conducted a poll in January, only 45 per cent had been found in favour, with 55 per cent against. By the end of March, 66 per cent of those polled were in favour with 34 per cent against.

It would be comforting to think the referendum result had been the product of a fully informed decision by a British people after a full public debate on the issue conducted by the contending parties. It was anything but. Not only were misleading statements made during the campaign by those supporting Britain's continued membership, but that side received far greater funding than did those campaigning for a 'no' vote. More gravely, there is evidence of covert CIA involvement to sway voters in favour of Britain's continued membership.

The Labour government itself was the source of the misleading statements in the campaign literature in support of Britain's continued membership. In the run-up to the referendum, voters had received three pieces of literature. One of the three documents had been produced by those campaigning on behalf of Britain remaining in the EEC. A second document had been produced by those campaigning against. Accompanying these two documents was a third document from the government which contained the following statements:

There was a threat to employment in Britain from the movement in the Common Market towards an Economic and Monetary Union. This would have forced us to accept fixed exchange rates for the pound, restricting industrial growth and so putting jobs at risk. That threat has been removed.

No important new policy can be decided in Brussels or anywhere else without the consent of a British Minister answerable to a British government and British Parliament... the Minister representing Britain can veto any proposals for a new law or new tax if he considers it to be against British interest.[40]

Of these two statements in the government-produced leaflet, Peter Shore observed: 'Both these statements, read today, are self-evidently untrue... though they were not flagrantly false in 1975... The... great difficulty that the European Union poses is... [that given its] aim of "ever-closer" union... the game is constantly changing... [W]hat was true thirty, twenty, or ten years ago is not necessarily what it is today.'[41]

The size of the mismatch in funding received by the two opposing campaign groups was staggering: 'Both the pro- and anti-EU campaigns enjoyed access to government grants of £125,000 for publicity. However, Britain in Europe [the organisation which united most of the pro-EU forces] managed to raise an additional £1.8 million from business and other sources, whereas the National Referendum Campaign [which brought together opponents of the EU] merely secured an extra £8,610.'[42]

The extra support received by those campaigning for Britain to remain in the EEC was not just financial. As political scientists Andy Mullen and Brian Burkitt have noted:

The civil service was not neutral during the referendum campaign. In addition to helping to produce the government's pamphlet, Whitehall assisted a number of task forces and liaison committees to support the 'Yes' campaign... The EU intervened in the referendum campaign through its British commissioners, prompting one commentator to remark that, in the deployment of two international civil servants, the pro-EU campaigners displayed an extraordinary lack of sensitivity to the constitutional ethics of non-interference in the domestic politics of a nation-state. It was also alleged that the Central Intelligence Agency intervened.[43]

The latter allegation was also made by former Conservative MP Richard Body, at the time of the referendum joint chairman of the Get Britain Out Council. As Body recounts in his 2001 book *England for the English*:

That Uncle Sam took active steps to ensure Britain was 'in Europe' is now an irrefutable fact. After I became joint chairman of the Get Britain Out Council, two Americans came to see me in 1975 with a large bundle of papers. They were, so they claimed, CIA agents who deplored their country's methods of interfering in the affairs of a good ally. What they had brought me were copies of documents which showed that a dedicated federalist, Cord Meyer Jr., was to become head of the CIA station in London for the duration of the Referendum 'to do what it takes' to secure a 'Yes' vote in favour of Britain remaining in the EEC. The papers showed that the CIA had already given the European Movement considerable sums of money, but now multinational corporations which had been assisted by the CIA were to be persuaded to fund the 'Yes' campaign through indirect channels.[44]

In his 1981 autobiography *Facing Reality: From World Federalism to the Central Intelligence Agency* Meyer confirms that he was the CIA's London Station Chief during this period.[45]

When it manoeuvred for Britain to join and stay in the EEC, America might well have thought it was cunningly planting a Trojan horse within Europe to ensure that it would remain friendly towards the United States. The reality instead could well be that America had unwittingly sacrificed its closest European ally that could soon be swallowed up a Germany-dominated European Union with a foreign policy agenda different to America's and deeply inimical to its geo-political interests. That scenario should be as unwelcome to America as undoubtedly it would be to Britain.

The historical excursions in this chapter into the origins and rationale of the EU, and into how and why Britain came to join it, place an altogether different gloss on these matters from that commonly placed on them by those in favour of Britain's EU membership. Whenever membership of the EU is said to be contrary to Britain's best interests, those in favour of its EU membership invariably respond by contending that any such suggestion is motivated either by erroneous economic suppositions or else by morally questionable, outmoded and chauvinistic nationalist sentiment. In the two chapters that now follow, I will consider in turn the arguments of those who make these claims. I will seek to show that, for reasons entirely unconnected with the somewhat murky origins of the EU, it was never in Britain's national interest to have joined or in its present interest to remain part of it, however much membership of it might conceivably be to the advantage of its other member states.

2

The Economic Costs and Benefits of Membership

Those who favour Britain's membership of the EU typically adduce on its behalf two principal sets of consideration: economic and political. The economic considerations are all essentially variations on a single theme, as are the political ones.

In the case of the economic considerations, their essential theme is that of the profound economic benefits EU membership allegedly confers on its member states by providing them with unimpeded access to the markets of other members. In the case of the political considerations, their essential theme is that, in an increasingly globalised and interdependent world, sovereign nation states are becoming atavistic, outmoded and divisive. Today's problems demand more supra-national forms of governance for their solution.

To understand how central these considerations are to the case for Britain's membership of the EU, consider the following account of 'the meaning of Maastricht' by Ernest Wistrich, for twenty years Director of the European Movement in Britain. He begins his 1994 book *The United States of Europe* thus:

> Over the last half century... dramatic changes... have thrown up new problems that can no longer be tackled by individual countries... Unfettered national sovereignty is obsolete...

When the Treaty of Rome established the European Economic Community in 1958 one of its objectives was to set up a common market without customs barriers, primarily to improve the living standards of its citizens. The creation of the Common Market had dramatic results. Between 1958 and 1972 the economies of the six member states of the Community grew much faster than that of the USA... The progressive removal of the customs barriers and the development of closer economic relations between member states stimulated growth and accelerated the growth of living standards throughout the Community... But an integrated market would not endure without the removal of... separate national currencies and the lack of a clear common voice with outside countries. That is why... the [1986 Single European] Act called for progress to economic and monetary union and the extension of the Community's responsibilities to foreign policy and security.[1]

The economic benefits that Wistrich claims the EU confers on its members form but the appetiser. Its real and main benefits, so he claims, are political, not economic:

The goal of common security was... the main motivating force behind the decision of the European countries... to unite... Interdependence... has made war between its members not only unthinkable but no longer practicable. Europe's living standards... largely depend on the preservation of peace in the rest of the world... This is why... the European Community needs a single foreign policy that actively pursues its common interests... It is in this context that the Community's... commitment to... [a] Common Foreign and Security Policy is so important... Growing economic interdependence within regions and between them would lay the foundations for a world free from local or general wars. Common global

problems such as the protection of the environment...
would be easier to pursue... From there, the next step
could be to provide the whole of our planet with a system
of enforceable international law under the authority of a
world government with strictly limited but real powers.[2]

Conspicuous in this last quotation are the globalist
aspirations of so many, like Wistrich, who champion
the European Union. However, it is by appealing to the
economic and security interests of its member states that
they primarily argue for its benefits. What needs now to
be identified and then subjected to critical scrutiny are
the specific considerations that these supporters of the
EU typically adduce on behalf of their contention that
EU membership does confer significant economic and
political benefits upon its member states. The present
chapter examines the alleged economic benefits; the
following chapter the alleged political benefits.

The alleged economic benefits of EU membership

Supporters of the European project make a series of claims
on behalf of their contention that the EU benefits the
economies of its member states. The single market, they
say, boosts commerce and supports millions of jobs by
eliminating tariff barriers and by harmonising regulations
so that the same commodity can be sold everywhere
within the EU effortlessly.[3] This, in turn, increases
competition, market size, and diversity, thus benefitting
the consumer in terms of price and choice. The increase
in exports and activity translates into substantial GDP
growth – figures as high as five per cent of GDP are cited
in the media.[4]

Furthermore, pro-Europeans contend that the size of
the single market (500 million people, and an affluent
500 million at that) makes the EU especially enticing as an
investment prospect, so that membership boosts inwards

foreign direct investment (FDI). They cite Japanese car manufacturers (UK) and Apple (Republic of Ireland) as examples of large international companies investing heavily within the EU.[5]

This size and attractiveness, argues the Confederation for British Industry (CBI), means that the EU has augmented 'clout' for negotiating free trade deals with other large or important world players. Only with Europe's great size, so they claim, could China, India, Japan or the USA be impressed into negotiating a trade deal. If Britain tried this alone, she would either be ignored or forced into signing a lopsided deal.

There are more specific claims, too. Financial services centres, not least the City of London, may be more profitable because of free movement rules on services and capital which, thanks to 'banking passports', ensure respect of mutual standards.[6] Finally, the role that the EU has played in peaceful relations is said to provide a stable, even cordial, atmosphere for business activity to flourish.[7]

For all of these perceived benefits, EU supporters argue that the price to Britain of its EU membership (below) has been a small one:

UK government gross and net payments to the EU from 2007 to 2013 in £million

	2007	2008	2009	2010	2011	2012	2013*
GROSS PAYMENTS	12,456	12,653	14,129	15,197	15,357	15,746	17,184
NET CONTRIBUTIONS	4,601	3,294	4,336	7,382	8,082	8,468	8,624

*2013 figures are estimates. Net figure adjusted for EU spending in the UK and the 'British Abatement' (AKA 'rebate')[8]

Optimistic evaluations of EU economics are usually delivered without evidence, or with bare scraps. The

CBI, for example, produced a report in 2013 to set out its EU position. It was over 180 pages long and repeated ad nauseum the claim that Britain's membership was worth £1,225 per capita. This figure, which was splashed across headlines and summaries, emerged from their calculation that EU membership was worth four to five per cent of GDP, or £62–78 billion.[9]

How did the CBI calculate this bold economic statement? Via complicated econometric modelling showing how Britain might have developed outside the single market? By comparison with countries similar to Britain but without any arrangement similar to EU membership? No, the CBI derived this central claim from a 'review of literature' which compared five old studies, one a decade out of date. However, one of these studies found that the EU hampered Britain's economy, and it seems to have been ignored in favour of Boltho and Eichengreen's research which found a five per cent GDP benefit for a generic member state (i.e. not Britain specifically) and admitted to a very large margin of error.[10] There was no explanation for the CBI's selection of 'credible analyses' or how they chose four to five per cent, when even most of the positive studies they reviewed found only a 2.0–2.5 per cent boost.

Eurosceptics have been rather more thorough in challenging the single market's benefits, and in questioning the worth of that annual £8.6 billion price tag in the form of Britain's net contribution to the EU budget.

Michael Burrage, writing for Civitas, tested pro-European ideas of an 'insider advantage' by comparing Britain's export success with that of comparably developed economies, both inside and outside Europe. Using extensive UN (Conference on Trade and Development) and OECD data, he found that, while there may have been a slight benefit to joining the 'common market' in 1973 in terms of sales to the continent, this quickly evaporated, while the 'single market' of the 1990s onwards had no observable benefits. It may well be holding Britain back, since non-EU countries seem to be expanding sales to continental countries faster.[11]

Likewise, Roger Bootle, founder of *Capital Economics* and winner of the Wolfson Economics Prize, judged Brussels' claims to success harshly in *The Trouble with €urope*. Bootle argues that the EU's robust growth in the 1960s was more a recovery from World War II and an urban transformation than a validation of the common market. He further suggests that poor governance, overemphasis on labour protection and over-harmonisation, plus an absence of intergovernmental competition, now hold back the EU as a whole.[12] He sees no great danger in Britain's leaving: even the worst case scenario would simply be trading with the EU under the same conditions as successful countries like China, Japan and the USA.

Specifically examining regulation, the think-tank Open Europe used UK government 'Impact Assessments' to determine that EU regulations cost Britain over £19 billion in 2009. Similarly, UKIP's economist Tim Congdon has investigated the impact of prominently damaging EU laws and quantified their impact as being almost £50 billion per year.[13] Elsewhere, an IEA study estimated that the price distortions and protectionism of the Common Agricultural Policy meant that UK food prices are 17 per cent higher than they need to be,[14] while a recent Taxpayers' Alliance investigation found the Common Fisheries Policy cost Britain £2.8 billion annually, with the added 'bonus' of decimating fish stocks, perhaps irreparably.[15]

The claim that Britain needs EU 'clout' to secure free trade deals is similarly misleading. Burrage's study touches on Switzerland which is not an EU member and has an economy far smaller than Britain's, although it is similarly advanced. He found that Switzerland, brokering free trade deals alone, had: (i) more deals than the EU, which (ii) had been signed faster, (iii) were more comprehensive, and (iv) opened far more impressive markets.[16] Swiss deals included those with China, Hong Kong, Canada and Japan, none of whom has a trade deal with the EU at present. This means that Swiss companies have tariff-free access to markets worth $19,541.7 billion, compared to the EU's $758.624 billion. Moreover, Swiss deals often include the free sale of services which EU deals omit.[17] Roger Bootle discusses this issue too, noting that Britain cannot join 'NAFTA' (a free trade area with Mexico, Canada and America) due to current EU rules.

A further Burrage study looks into the claim that the single market attracts extra FDI. Burrage again shows that common market entry may have caused a temporary spike in investment, but over the long term EU membership seems to give member states little or no advantage compared with similar non-EU states. Recently Iceland, Switzerland and Norway (none of which are full EU members) considerably outperformed the EU, even controlling for Norway's oil and Switzerland's banking sectors.[18]

The City's stance on the EU is mixed. The think tank Global Britain hosts events for financial service industry representatives who are very critical of Brussels. It recently published a study arguing that the City will prosper without the EU's regulatory millstone.[19]

As examples of EU regulation which hurts London, critics of the EU highlight many of its initiatives, such as the bonus cap for bankers, the requirement for euro trading houses to be based in the eurozone and the Financial Transaction Tax. A 2012 report commissioned by the CBI itself fears that proposed pension changes would impose £350 billion costs on UK businesses and hit long-term growth by 2.5 per cent of GDP.[20]

One of the most comprehensive attempts to quantify the economic costs to Britain of its membership of the EU was that undertaken for the IEA by Patrick Minford and two research associates from the Cardiff Business School, published in 2005 under the title *Should Britain Leave the EU?* They estimated that the costs to Britain were somewhere between 11.2 and 37.7 per cent of its annual GDP. The main source of these costs, as well as reason for the uncertainty as to their precise magnitude, was the steady volume of regulation that has flown relentlessly from Brussels.

When the Minford report was published, its authors could hardly have been expected to have foreseen three major subsequent developments within the EU that have each been severely detrimental to Britain economically-speaking. The first such development were the extremely ambitious targets that the EU set its member states for reducing their carbon emissions and for increasing their use of renewable sources of energy by 2020. The second development has been the welter of legislation that has flowed from Brussels since the global financial crisis of 2008 designed to regulate banking and the financial services within the EU and which has hit, or else threatens to hit, the City of London particularly hard. The third development has been the massive influx to Britain of migrants from former communist bloc countries after their accession to the EU beginning in 2004. The adverse effect on Britain of these three developments will now be explained.

The costs to Britain of the EU's climate-change policies

By the time that the Minford report was published, there were already enough straws in the wind to suggest that the EU would, in the near future, be greatly adding to the economic costs of Britain's membership through ostensible environmental concerns. As Sheffield University's professor of politics Andrew Geddes has noted: 'Environmental policy... ascended the EU agenda in the 1970s, reflective of increased concern about "post-material" quality of life issues. Environmental policy was formalized as an EU competence by the Maastricht Treaty, while Amsterdam enshrined the principle of sustainable development.'[21]

In accord with that competence, the EU was, along with the UK and other member states, a signatory in June 1992 to the United Nations Framework Convention on Climate Change (UNFCCC), agreed immediately following the so-called 'Earth Summit' in Rio de Janeiro. The treaty committed signatories to combatting global warming, a commitment that gained teeth with the Kyoto Protocol in 1997 that bound them to a set of reduction targets for greenhouse gas (GHG) emissions that were finalised in the so-called 'Marrakech Accords' of 2001.

In signing the Kyoto Protocol, industrialised countries committed themselves to reducing GHG emissions by 2012 to five per cent below their 1990 levels and by a further 18 per cent by 2020. The Kyoto Protocol came into force in February 2005, the same month as the Minford report was published. Its authors, therefore, could hardly have been expected to have realised with just how sharp a set of teeth the Kyoto Protocol had equipped environmentalism. Not until 2008, when the EU unveiled its Climate Action and Renewable Energy Package (CAREP), did Britain and other member states learn how the EU had decided they would each have to meet their GHG emission reduction targets.

CAREP consisted of four new directives which, at the time, EC President José Manuel Barroso heralded as being 'the most far-reaching set of legislative proposals by the European Commission for many years'. By the end of 2008, the four directives had all been transposed into statutes by member states that came into effect in June 2009.

What the four CAREP directives required of EU member states was that, by 2020, each should have reduced overall GHG emissions by 20 per cent below their 1990 levels, largely through mandatory participation in a centrally administered carbon Emissions Trading Scheme (ETS). Each member state received a centrally allocated tradable carbon allowance that it could then either use or else sell to another member state. Additionally, by 2020, each member state was required by the EU to have started to derive 20 per cent of its energy supplies from renewable sources of energy such as solar power and wind. To achieve that objective, each member state was centrally assigned a specific energy-mix target. Finally, through greater energy efficiency, each member state was also expected to have reduced energy consumption by 2020 to 20 per cent below its previously projected level.

At both its UN and EU level, the entire GHG emissions reduction programme has been predicated on the assumption that, ever since the Industrial Revolution, global temperatures have been increasing at a dangerously fast pace, and that, unless GHG emissions can be brought back to sustainable levels through the concerted efforts of world governments, the planet faced an ever-growing risk of ecological catastrophe through anthropogenic global warming. Those who favour the global imperative to reduce carbon emissions claim that it is based on unassailable scientific evidence, first, that, for many past decades, global temperatures have been rising, and, second, that a good part of this warming is anthropogenic, meaning caused by GHG emissions from the burning of fossil fuels, largely coal, oil, and gas.

It is possible to question the evidential basis of both these presuppositions behind the Kyoto Protocol, as it is to question the notion that the best means at humanity's disposal for dealing with global warming, assuming both presuppositions correct, is through seeking to abate GHG emissions rather than adapting to higher global temperatures.[22] As long as both these presuppositions remain as widely accepted as they currently are, however, economically developed countries like Britain will have little option but to seek to reduce GHG emissions. Assuming the reasonableness, or at least the unavoidability, of their having to do this, it is still open to question whether the scheme to lower these emissions that the EU has foisted upon its member states is the most efficient that it could have chosen.

Admittedly, the UK has no need of assistance from the EU when it comes to imposing needlessly expensive environmental policies which are of dubious efficacy. Towards the end of November 2008, the Westminster Parliament pre-empted the EU by enacting a Climate Change Act with all-party support that committed Britain to reducing its greenhouse gas emissions by 2050 to 'at least 80 per cent' below their 1990 level. Not until December 2011 did the EU set other member states a similar target. Of the passing of the 2008 Climate Change Act, Nigel Lawson has aptly remarked: 'This may well go down in history as the most absurd piece of legislation any British parliament has passed.'[23] It may do so, because it will prove colossally expensive for Britain to meet this target which, in any case, will have only the tiniest impact on abating global GHG emissions. The same holds true of the EU's 2050 targets.

Were Britain outside the EU, a future British government would find it much easier to correct such a misguided policy after its costliness and ineffectiveness had become fully apparent. This is especially so, given how different its energy needs and resources are from those of other members.

No organisation has sought more painstakingly to

estimate the costs of the EU's environmental policies to Britain than Open Europe. In October 2008, it published a study of these likely costs. It concluded that they would be more than double the European Commission's estimate: £9 billion per annum, plus a further £2.5 billion with grid connecting costs, as against the EC's estimate of £4.4-£6.3 billion per annum.[24] Among member states, only Germany, with a larger population and higher energy consumption than Britain, would face higher costs.

The main reason that the environmental policies of the EU will prove so costly to Britain is that, by 2020, the EU is requiring Britain to have increased the share of renewable sources of energy in its energy mix from 1.3 per cent to 15 per cent. This is the highest percentage increase required of any member state. Were Britain to leave the EU, and hence become capable of taking its own decisions on how to set about lowering its GHG emissions, it could easily achieve the target without increasing its use of renewable energy sources by anything like as much. As well as being notoriously unreliable, renewable sources of energy are far more expensive than are several non-renewable alternatives. Meeting EU demands will make British industry less competitive internationally than it need be.

Moreover, as Open Europe noted in 2008, an emissions trading scheme is a far less effective way to reduce GHG emission levels than a simple carbon tax. By making GHG emission allowances tradable, as well as by granting certain exemptions, this scheme has left several ways open to EU member states, not simply to avoid reducing their GHG emissions, but even to increase them with impunity. One such loophole is provided by the so-called Clean Development Mechanism. This enables EU countries to purchase credits for GHG emissions from abroad by contributing financially towards the GHG emissions reduction schemes of less developed countries. The loophole has been exploited by some of the EU's heaviest CHG emitters. As David Craig and Matthew Elliott noted in their 2009 book on the short-comings of the EU, *The Great European Rip-Off*: 'Germany, for example, "yielded" to pressure from the Commission to reduce its CO_2 cap by 28.9 million tonnes a year for 2007–13 but extracted as compensation an increase in its import allowance of 32.8 million tonnes a year, about 213 per cent more than it had given up... In reality, the many loopholes in importing credits from the Third World and other ways of cheating the scheme will probably mean that the EU ETS never has any effect on EU CO_2 emissions at all.'[25]

The ETS scheme has been further undermined by the collapse in the market for GHG emission permits, precipitated, first, by the global economic recession that began in 2008, and, second, by the American shale gas revolution. Both economic phenomena have led to a very steep reduction in the world price of coal, to which Germany has responded by vastly increasing its reliance on this energy source after deciding, in the wake of the Fukushima disaster of March 2011, to phase out all its nuclear reactors by 2020. As was reported in August 2012: 'Germany's largest utilities... are shunning cleaner-burning natural gas because it's more costly, while the collapsing cost of carbon permits means that there's little penalty for burning coal... The price of carbon dioxide permits in the European Union has dropped 43 per cent over the past year... European Union carbon emissions may rise 43 million metric tons this year because of increased coal burning at power stations...'[26]

As Open Europe observed in its submission to the Government's current Competences Review, the European Union would have been able to set developing countries that are very heavy emitters of GHG a much better environmental example were it to have encouraged truly cost effective ways of reducing their emission.[27]

Instead, it has advocated the greater use of prohibitively expensive renewable sources of energy. In view of its turn to coal, Open Europe might have added, Germany could have helped to set such an example by practising what it was, in vain, preaching to countries like India, China, and Brazil, for all of whom environmental concerns such as these remain idle luxuries.

The costs to Britain of the EU's regulation of financial services

Besides helping to revive the use of coal in industry, the 2008 financial crash and ensuing global recession have led to one other significant development within the EU. They have provided it with an opportunity, long and eagerly awaited in some quarters, to begin to regulate financial services and banking. The multifarious ways in which it has begun to do so threaten to prove especially costly for Britain, given the importance of financial services in its economy. In December 2011, Open Europe stated that: 'The financial services industry is vital to the UK economy. In the 2009/10 tax year [it]... made a total contribution of... 11.2 per cent of the Government's total tax receipts for that year. Financial services... in 2010 [were] the only industry sector in the UK that generated a substantial surplus apart from "other business services", many of which are closely linked to financial services.'[28]

A year before Open Europe published its report, the German economist Roland Vaubel had warned Britain how damaging the EU's new regulatory regime was liable to be to its financial services sector. He contended the damage was not accidental, saying: 'Under qualified majority voting, the majority of highly regulated countries (say, France) have an incentive and power to impose their high level of regulation on the minority of more market-oriented countries (say, the UK) in order to weaken the latter's competitiveness... Following the financial crisis, the French government has pursued the strategy of raising rivals' costs in a deliberate and consistent manner.'[29]

In support of his contention that the new EU regulatory scheme was intended to undermine Britain's financial services, Vaubel cited a remark made in November 2009 by the then French President Nicholas Sarkozy about his compatriot Michel Barnier shortly after Barnier's appointment as EC Commissioner for the Internal Market: 'Do you know what it means for me to see for the first time in fifty years a French European Commissioner in charge of the internal market, including financial services, including the City [of London]? I want the world to see the victory of the European model, which has nothing to do with the excesses of financial capitalism.'[30] The British press reported, shortly before Barnier's rumoured appointment, that: 'Mr Barnier... has a track record of hostility to the "Anglo-Saxon" free market model of capitalism. Britain fears that, if he takes a full blooded internal market portfolio, including financial services, then the City will face heavy regulations on private equity and hedge funds, damaging the British economy.'[31]

British fears about what the new EC Commissioner might do in that office appear to have been fully justified. Shortly after Barnier took up his appointment, Brussels issued an array of directives and regulations subjecting financial markets in the EU to a new regulatory regime modelled on the uniquely French 'three-peaked approach'. These regulations and directives have placed financial services within the EU under three new supervisory authorities: a European Banking Authority based in London; a European Securities and Markets Authority based in Paris; and a European Insurance and Occupational Pensions Authority based in Frankfurt. Along with these three new supervisory authorities, the EU has also issued multifarious new directives and regulations in the name of subjecting financial services and banking within it to greater harmonisation and tighter control. This new mass of EU law has subjected these industries to a vast panoply of costly new mandatory procedures and requirements, for which, in the case of Britain at least, there is arguably little need, save to render its financial services sector internationally uncompetitive.

Altogether, Brussels has placed, or is in process of placing, no fewer than six new regulatory burdens on financial services within the EU, each of which is liable to prove disproportionately costly to Britain. These six-fold burdens are: first, the capping of the bonuses of bankers and fund managers; second, a proposed financial transaction tax; third, a new policy for clearing houses handling 'sizable' amounts of euro-denominated business requiring their relocation to within the eurozone; fourth, new solvency requirements for insurance companies; fifth, a new regime for occupational pensions schemes; and, finally, a new directive pertaining to investment fund management known as the 'Alternative Investment Fund Managers Directive'.

As yet, it is still too early to quantify what the costs of all these new measures will be for Britain. In each case, however, its likely cost has been forecast to be substantial by those with expert opinion in the relevant area. To gain some notion of how much damage these new burdens are liable to inflict on Britain's financial services should it continue to remain within the EU, it is worth briefly considering the predicted cost of each.

1. Cap on bankers' bonuses
The EU now requires that the maximum annual bonuses paid to bankers based anywhere within the EU be no greater than a year of their salary, or a maximum of twice their annual pay if the bonus is backed by a majority

of shareholders. The CBI's chief policy officer Katja Hall has commented: 'The proposals will damage the competitiveness of the EU's financial services industry, hitting the UK particularly hard, at a time when growth should be the key priority.'[32]

Likewise, Adrian Kinnersley, managing director of the City recruiting firm Twenty Recruitment has warned that, if instituted, the banking cap would inflict severe damage on the City of London: 'This will be seen by many organisations as the final regulatory straw and encourage institutions to relocate their headquarters overseas and take talent, tax revenues and income with them. The figures speak for themselves – if we lose that tax revenue then our economy is finished. The latest move, combined with the Tobin [Financial Transaction] Tax makes running a financial services business in Europe extremely uncompetitive when compared with the US and Asia which have not gone as far.'[33]

2. *Financial transactions tax*

What Adrian Kinnersley colloquially refers to as a Tobin Tax is a new tax that the EU is currently seeking to levy upon all financial transactions that meet either of two qualifying conditions. The first is that one party be based in one of eleven EU member states that have agreed to its imposition, under a provision of the Lisbon Treaty known as the Enhanced Cooperation Procedure (ECP). The second is that a financial transaction has concerned some financial product originating in one of these eleven countries.

The ECP allows as few as nine member states to create such advanced forms of integration and cooperation, provided that they do not impinge on other member states. Given the volume of transactions conducted daily by Britain's financial services that would meet these qualifying conditions for the new proposed tax, the FTT would clearly impinge greatly on the City. This has led Britain to challenge the legality of the proposed tax before the European Court of Justice, but without success.

Speaking at a meeting of EU finance ministers in early May 2014, shortly after the ECJ rejected the UK's appeal against the FTT, Britain's Chancellor of the Exchequer George Osborne condemned the proposed new tax, saying: 'It's not a tax on bankers, it's a tax on jobs, on investment, on people's pensions. That's why the United Kingdom does not want to be a part of it. If they seek to damage jobs and investment across the rest of Europe, then we are entitled to challenge that. We have a situation where 11 member states are working up their proposals, largely in secret, and we get a piece of paper handed to us all saying "Oh this, by the way, is what we've agreed".' [34]

It is unlikely that the European Commission will heed Britain's objections to the new tax. EU taxation commissioner Algirdas Semeta responded to Chancellor Osborne's lament: 'We should be clear that the ECJ rejected UK's challenge on the FTT. This should pave the way for its adoption.'[35]

The European Commission originally proposed the new tax in 2011, partly as a way to raise revenue, since the revenue it yields is intended to go to Brussels, not the member states where it will be collected. The new tax was also proposed to curb what many in the European Union consider to have been frivolous transactions by traders whose excesses many have deemed responsible for the financial crisis of 2008.

When the EC first proposed a Europe-wide tax on all financial transactions within the EU, Britain and Luxembourg were able to veto it, as they then had power to do so. In its current proposed form, the tax has been revived by the 11 member states who would like to see it imposed in a way that precludes other member states from being able to veto it.

Should the proposed tax be instituted, Britain's financial services will be very adversely affected. To avoid it, trading companies which have previously been located in the City of London will simply move their operations to centres outside of the EU. Should they not move, the UK government would be likely to oblige these traders to raise the tax upon trades that met the conditions, since otherwise the UK would be liable for an EU fine.

Alex van der Velden is a partner and chief investment officer at the Amsterdam-based asset management firm Ownership Capital and former head of responsible equity strategies at Dutch pensions firm PGGM. He has remarked of the proposed tax that: 'Given the size of the market in the European Union and the amount of foreign investment here, this has the potential to become a real issue for the continent's competitiveness on a global level.'[36]

When news reports broke of a leaked document showing that the EU's own lawyers considered the proposed tax of dubious legality, an editorial welcoming the news in the Business Section of the *Daily Telegraph* stated that: 'its cost could cut GDP growth by as much as 0.3 per cent across the EU... This wrong-headed tax is just the latest in a series of similar attacks by stealth on the UK's position. In fact, too many of the financial regulations proposed by the EU over recent years have seemed more focused on undermining the UK's hard-won position as the leading financial centre in Europe than with any serious attempt at increasing the security of the global banking system.'[37]

Germany is one of the 11 EU member states sponsoring the proposed new tax. It remained unmoved by news of the leaked document. In response to the leak, the German government issued a statement signalling its continuing support for the tax by declaring: 'The German government advocates a swift introduction of the FTT for good reasons. We want to make the financial sector contribute adequately to the costs of the financial crisis. Nothing has changed on that. The legal concerns must be cleared up and dispelled as quickly as possible.'[38]

3. ECB location policy for clearing houses with 'sizable' euro-denominated trades

One of the functions assigned by the Lisbon Treaty to the European Central Bank (ECB) was to 'promote the smooth operations of payment systems' used to settle euro-denominated transactions. In July 2007, the ECB set out what it called 'Policy principles on the location and operation of infrastructures settling payment transactions'. One of the principles was that: 'Payment infrastructures settling euro-denominated payment transactions that have the potential to reach systemic relevance for the euro area should… be incorporated in the euro area.'[39]

At the time these principles were issued, the ECB left it unclear how large transactions would have to be before they could be considered of systemic relevance. In July 2011, however, the ECB published a so-called 'Eurosystem Oversight Policy Framework' which shed ominous further light on the matter so far as British financial interests are concerned. The document stated:

> Given its mandate to promote the 'smooth operations of payment systems', the Eurosystem has major concerns with regard to the development of major euro financial markets… located outside of the euro area… As a matter of principle, infrastructures that settle euro-denominated payment transactions should… be legally incorporated in the euro area … [O]ffshore CCPs [clearing houses] … that on average have a daily net credit exposure of more than €5 billion in one of the main euro-denominated product categories… should be legally incorporated

in the euro area with full managerial and operational control and responsibility over all core functions[for processing euro denominated transactions] exercised from within the euro area. [40]

The ECB's locations policy poses a major threat to the City of London. As IEA fellow Keith Boyfield explained in the *Wall Street Journal*: 'London is by far the leading player in euro-denominated financial markets... London currently clears trades worth several billions of euros each year through four central counterparty clearing houses (CCPs). They compete with [three] main eurozone CCPs... [which] would like to win the euro-denominated business now undertaken in London... Loss of its euro-clearing capability would be a serious blow to London.'[41]

The British government is currently challenging the ECB's location policy before the European Court of Justice on the grounds that it contravenes the principles of the Single Market. Who will finally prevail remains to be seen. Were Britain to lose its case, it would seem to matter little whether it continues to remain within the EU or leaves, since so much of any economic benefit it might derive from being a member would have been lost.

4. New solvency requirements for insurance companies

Britain's insurance industry forms a major component of its financial services sector and is a great asset to the country. According to the Association of British Insurers: 'The UK insurance industry is the third largest in the world and the largest in Europe... managing investments amounting to 26 per cent of the UK's total net worth and contributing £10.4 billion in taxes to the Government. Employing some 290,000 people in the UK alone, the insurance industry is also one of this country's major exporters, with almost 30 per cent of its net premium income coming from overseas business.'[42]

'Solvency II' is a proposed new set of regulatory requirements for the insurance industry emanating from Brussels. The requirements are ostensibly designed to safeguard consumer interests by restraining insurance providers from over-exposing themselves to risk in the management of their investment portfolios.

The proposed new requirements threaten to raise costs and insurance premiums, thereby reducing the international competitiveness of the industry. So cumbersome and potentially threatening to the industry are the new proposed regulatory requirements that, in February 2013, Andrew Bailey, managing director of the Bank of England's Prudential Regulation Authority, wrote a letter to the chairman of the Treasury Select Committee informing him of his concerns. In that letter, subsequently made public, the head of the UK's new financial services regulator described Solvency II as 'lost in detail and vastly expensive'. Their implementation costs, he stated, would be 'staggering'. When asked to elaborate on these claims, Bailey replied in a further public letter that he estimated annual compliance costs would amount to £200 million and lead to a 0.1 per cent increase in premiums.

The adverse impact that Solvency II is liable to have upon the UK's insurance industry was spelt out by John Hodgson, a former executive director of Norwich Union and Chief Operations and Transformations Officer for Aviva:

> There will now be large capital penalties if the regulator's position is not followed... Companies' balance sheets will become increasingly similar... stuffed with government bonds... with ever less risk taken... The lack of diversity in insurers' ability to manage risk also reduces customer choice and removes important sources of long-term finance from the economy, exposing the entire system to greater risk if either fundamental misjudgements

are made, or a novel source of risk, not anticipated in the regulatory imagination, emerges... The UK, and indeed European, insurance industry is, as a result... at a disadvantage in competing against US and emerging market competitors, with consequences for employment, growth and export earnings.[43]

5. Proposed new funding regime for occupational pensions

Undaunted by these concerns, the European Commission is now proposing, as a way of improving the security of private occupational pension schemes, a new, and very costly, Solvency II-inspired funding regime. According to an independent report for the CBI by the economic consultancy firm Oxford Economics, published in December 2012: 'the economic impact [of the scheme on Britain] would be profound and widespread.'[44] Using the UK as a case study to illustrate the impact the scheme is liable to have, the report estimates that:

◆ The additional call on UK businesses' funds could be in the order of €440 billion (£350 billion) – equivalent to an additional 7.9 per cent of affected firms' total employment costs for each of ten years.

◆ GDP would be 2.5 per cent lower in the mid-to-late 2020s than in the absence of any regime change, and would still be 0.6 per cent lower than otherwise in 2040.

◆ Business investment would be 5.2 per cent lower than otherwise in the mid-2020s, with a shortfall of 1.4 per cent still being felt in 2040.

◆ The average loss of GDP over the whole period 2022–40 would be 1.5 per cent, and, with the business sector capital stock 1.8 per cent smaller than otherwise in 2040, the path of GDP and productivity would remain weaker than otherwise going forward from there.

◆ Export volumes would fall short by 2.1 per cent in the mid-2020s due to reduced cost competitiveness, with subsequent revival dependent on currency depreciation and an associated squeeze on the typical household's spending power.

◆ Employment would fall short of where it would otherwise have been by 0.5 per cent, or 180,000, in the mid-2020s, with subsequent revival dependent on an additional squeeze on real wages.

◆ In the face of these pressures, consumer spending would be 2.0 per cent lower in real terms.[45]

The CBI has condemned the proposed changes as being wholly unneeded in the case of Britain. Katja Hall, CBI chief policy director, has said of them: 'We have a tough regulatory system in this country, so these changes are completely unnecessary. It's alarming the Commission is still turning a deaf ear to calls from businesses, trade unions and pension funds to bin these proposals.'[46]

6. The alternative investment fund managers directive (AIFMD)
This directive aims to regulate more closely the management of hedge funds and private equity firms within the EU. When it entered into force in July 2013, the directive was badly received by those who manage alternative funds in Britain. A survey conducted in 2012 by Deloitte found that: 'the vast majority of UK-based respondents, representing over £175 billion in investment funding, consider the AIFM directive a threat

to business... 68 per cent of respondents surveyed... expect that the compliance burden imposed by the regulations will reduce the industry's competitiveness.'[47]

According to Scott Cochrane, partner and regional head of Corporate at the legal firm Herbert Smith Freehills: 'For UK authorised managers, little if any of the additional requirements are obviously necessary from the perspective of protecting investors or ensuring a properly operating asset management industry... Industry sources put the incremental one-off costs of compliance at up to £1.6 million per firm with annual compliance costs increasing by up to £2.33 million per firm. The total costs across the EU of complying will therefore run into hundreds of millions over the next five years (with a significant proportion being borne by UK based firms).'[48]

The costs to Britain of immigration from the EU

Since 2005, the UK also incurred further substantial economic costs from its EU membership arising from the large number of migrants who have arrived from eight former communist-bloc countries in Eastern Europe since their accession to the EU in 2004. Britain could have decided, as did most other EU countries, to impose transitional requirements delaying by seven years the full employment rights of migrants from the A8 countries as these former communist countries were known. However, it chose not to. The result has been that, since 2004, the British labour market has been subject to a massive influx of migrants from these countries, an influx that is liable to be both prolonged and considerably augmented, as from the beginning of 2014, by migrants from Bulgaria and Romania.

When the New Labour government accorded migrants from the A8 countries immediate full employment rights, it justified its decision by claiming that the UK was suffering from an acute shortage of domestic labour.

In addition to filling vacancies that would otherwise have gone unfilled, it predicted, the resulting volume of inwards migration would not be excessively large and would hence prove a boon to the economy. In the event, there was much greater migration to Britain from these countries than had been predicted. The result has been that considerable strain has been placed on the country's infrastructure and public services, and, hence, on the public purse.

The economic costs to Britain of the large volume of migration that it has received from the EU as a result of its membership goes well beyond these infrastructural costs. Additionally, there is evidence that immigration from the A8 countries has led to a considerable amount of domestic unemployment, as British nationals have been displaced from jobs by EU migrants willing to work either for lower wages or in inferior conditions than their British counterparts. In his 2013 report on the costs of EU membership, economist Tim Congdon has provided a rough estimate of the cost to Britain of British-born workers experiencing job-displacement through open immigration from the EU. Congdon estimates the cost to have been 0.25 per cent of GDP per annum. He arrived at what he admits can only be a crude estimate of these costs on the basis of the impact that migration from A8 countries has had on the composition of the UK labour market since 2004. Using data from Office for National Statistics, Congdon first noted that:

Between March 2004 and the end of 2007... the number [of people born in the EUA8 employed in the UK] rose from 64,000 to 487,000. Within less than four years... they accounted for 1.7 per cent of total UK employment [having accounted for only 0.2 per cent in March 2004]. The growth of employment in this period for UK-born workers was only a little more than 100,000, a mere quarter of the surge of over 400,000 in employment of EUA8-born workers... In the Great Recession [that began in late 2007] and the immediately subsequent years, UK-born employment dropped heavily, whereas foreign-born employment rose and employment of people from the EUA8 climbed dramatically... The fall in UK-born employment... amounted to about 800,000 people, about three per cent of the number of UK-born people in jobs at the end of 2007... Employment of EUA8-born people soared by 45 per cent in the five years to end-2012... [T]he number of jobs occupied by the EUA8-born increased by 200,000... Until the 2004 enlargement, UK-resident people born in the EUA8 had an employment ratio *beneath* that of the UK-born... [I]n the four years from the first quarter of 2004... the employment ratio of the EUA8-born group soared from 61.9 per cent to 82.6 per cent... well above that of the UK-born... Further, when the Great Recession hit and the number of job opportunities declined, the immigrants did take jobs from the British-born. On this basis, EU membership *did* destroy UK jobs.[49]

Congdon then calculated the magnitude of the job-displacement effect that this large volume of inwards migration from the EU is likely to have had on British-born workers. He did so by drawing upon the claim, contained in a 2012 report by the Migration Advisory Committee, that an extra 160,000 British-born workers might have found jobs had there not been any non-EU immigration to Britain between 2005 and 2010. Congdon asks rhetorically: 'If immigration from *outside the EU* can reduce employment for British citizens, why cannot immigration *from within the EU* have the same effect?'[50] Assuming that it does, Congdon then inferred from official statistics concerning the numbers of EU and non-EU immigrants working in the UK between 2004 and

2011 what job displacement effect EU immigrant workers to the UK are likely to have had. According to official data, between 2005 and 2010, there was an increase of 652,000 in the number of non-EU workers working in Britain, and an increase of 588,000 EU workers working in Britain. From these figures, Congdon reasoned as follows: 'If the... [652,000] non-EU immigrant workers are supposed to have destroyed 160,000 jobs for the UK-born, then the 588,000 EU immigrant workers destroyed about 135,000 jobs for the UK-born.'[51] In a footnote, he explains how he then derived his estimate of the annual cost to Britain of inward migration from the EU as being almost 0.5 per cent of GDP. He writes: 'One calculation of the loss "to the UK" might... be the output that would have [been] expected from 135,000 people, if they had been in work and had had average UK productivity, which comes out at about £7 billion a year... The author is under few illusions about the fragility of the assumptions required to deliver this result.'[52]

That the UK will inevitably incur such losses in wealth as result of mass migration from poorer countries, such as those of the A8 and A2, was cogently demonstrated by Anthony Scholefield in a report published by the Social Affairs Unit in 2007 under the title *Warning: Immigration Can Seriously Damage Your Wealth*. The nub of Scholefield's argument runs thus:

> The core argument is that any addition to the population, whether through increased fertility or immigration without capital, must require capital and wealth to be provided for the newcomers. Either this is supplied by the newcomers alone (in which case, assuming wages similar to those of natives, they can never catch up with natives, who have already accumulated wealth) or it is appropriated from natives... and apportioned to newcomers, in which case the natives suffer a loss of

wealth. In one case, newcomers never catch up with natives and so cannot add to natives' wealth; in the other, the natives suffer an outright loss of wealth. The only exception to this… would be if newcomers were so skilled or so wealthy that they could provide for themselves the wealth the natives have accumulated over generations and centuries. Such newcomers to the USA and Britain do exist, but they are few in number. Only five out of 582,000 new arrivals in Britain in 2004 came under permits issued to persons 'of independent means'.[53]

From the beginning of 2014 migrants from Romania and Bulgaria have been eligible to work freely in the UK as well as qualifying for many attendant welfare benefits. Between April and June 2013, according to the Office for National Statistics, the number of Romanians and Bulgarians working in the UK rose by over a quarter, from 112,000 to 140,000.[54] In the first quarter of 2014, 45,000 new national insurance numbers were issued to Romanian and Bulgarian migrants of whom 10,000 had arrived in the UK in that quarter in line with Migrationwatch UK forecasts that their annual flow to Britain would now be 50,000.[55]

Open-door immigration from the EU is certainly a very big issue among British voters. UKIP leader Nigel Farage has predicted that it 'is going to become the number one issue when it comes to the referendum. Above everything else it is what people are going to vote on.'[56] Acutely aware of how many Conservative seats in Parliament risk being lost over the issue, Prime Minister David Cameron is seeking to introduce measures designed to contain costs and curb the number of immigrants by delaying their eligibility to housing and other welfare benefits, as well as by levying a charge for their use of the National Health Service in the case of non-EU immigrants. Certainly, the costs to Britain of immigration could do with being contained. A Home Office report has estimated that: 'On average, each migrant consumes between £5,050 and £8,350 per year in state services, including benefits, healthcare, schooling and social services.'[57]

The European Commission is strongly opposed to the measures that the British Government has proposed to curb the costs and numbers of migrants to Britain from the EU. Viviane Reding, EC Commissioner for Justice as well as Vice President of the EC, has said: 'If Britain wants to leave the single market, you should say so. But if Britain wants to stay a part of the single market, free movement applies. You cannot have your cake and eat it, Mr Cameron!'[58] Commissioner Reding has also been reported as saying: 'Don't blame the Commission or EU rules for national choices... If member states want to restrict the availability of social benefits to EU citizens they can... change their national systems to make them less generous.'[59]

3

The Political Costs and Benefits of Membership

The extra external security EU membership allegedly confers on its members

In these financially straitened times, the primary public concern in Britain about the high levels of immigration from the EU relate to job-displacement, plus the strain being placed on the public purse and infrastructure. In earlier decades, however, these public concerns about immigration to Britain were neither the only nor even the most pressing ones. In 1978, three years after she became leader of the Conservative Party, Margaret Thatcher was undoubtedly speaking for many of her compatriots when she remarked in a television interview, albeit with immigration to Britain from the Indian sub-continent primarily in mind:

> People are really rather afraid that this country might be rather swamped by people with a different culture and... if there is any fear that it might be swamped, people are going to react and be rather hostile to them coming in. So... you have got to allay people's fears on numbers. Now, the key to this... [is that] we must hold out the clear prospect of an end to immigration... except, of course, for compassionate cases... You see, my great fear is... that if [it continues at its present] rate... we shall not have good... relations with those who are here. Everyone who is here must be treated equally under the

law, and that, I think, is why quite a lot of them too are fearful that their position might be put in jeopardy or people might be hostile to them unless we cut down the incoming numbers. They are here. They are here. They must be treated equally.[1]

In 1978, the main public concern in Britain about immigration might well have been the cultural differences between a large proportion of migrants and the host population. Today, concern is more likely to focus on the threat that migrants pose to jobs, housing and public services. Whatever its source, unless such concern is adequately addressed, it will always provide a clear potential basis for social unrest.

Upon her party's return to government in 1979, Margaret Thatcher quickly addressed these concerns. New restrictions on immigration were swiftly imposed that enjoyed a wide measure of cross-party support until the New Labour government lifted them soon after its electoral victory in 1997. In any case, the concerns about immigration voiced by Thatcher long antedated the widening of the EU which has come to include millions of relatively impoverished East Europeans. With the eventual prospect of the accession to the EU of Turkey, whose citizens would thus acquire immigration and employment rights in Britain, cultural and economic concerns about mass migration are set to coalesce unless Britain decides to leave the EU.

Many will be inclined to dismiss all such concerns about mass migration to Britain as no more than a visceral xenophobia unworthy of serious consideration. Some will be inclined to view these concerns as no more than symptoms of a petty-minded nationalism which the EU was expressly designed to end. However much Europe's populations may have to adjust themselves mentally to accommodate each other's newly established propinquity, and however uncomfortable and disquieting such mutual adjustment might prove in the short to medium term, many will regard the discomfort as the unavoidable and worthwhile price of a Union which they consider to be the only way to prevent recurrence of war between the peoples of Europe. Indeed, many of the EU's most fervent champions have viewed this as its primary purpose. Winston Churchill advocated European Union on precisely these grounds, although he explicitly excluded Britain from the need to join in the project. Speaking at the University of Zurich in 1946, he said:

> It is from Europe that have sprung that series of frightful nationalistic quarrels... which we have seen in this twentieth century... Yet all the while there is a remedy which... would as if by a miracle... in a few years make all Europe... as free and happy as Switzerland is today. What is this sovereign remedy? It is to re-create the European family... and to provide it with a structure under which it can dwell in peace, in safety and in freedom. We must build a kind of United States of Europe.[2]

Shortly after the creation of the ECSC, West Germany's Chancellor Konrad Adenauer repeated Churchill's thesis declaring that: 'The age of national states has come to an end... We in Europe must break ourselves of the habit of thinking in terms of national states... European agreements... are intended to make war among European nations impossible in future... If the idea of European community should survive for fifty years, there will never again be a European war...'[3] The thesis was to be repeated several decades later by another Christian Democrat German Chancellor, Helmut Kohl. Speaking at the Catholic University of Leuven in 1996, Kohl famously remarked that: 'the policy of European integration is a matter of war and peace in the twenty-first century... The nation-state of the nineteenth century cannot solve the great problems of the twenty-first century. Nationalism brought suffering to our continent.'[4]

More recently, the same notion has been repeated, first, by EU Council President Herman Van Rompuy: 'We have together to fight the danger of a new Euroscepticism... The biggest enemy of Europe today is fear. Fear leads to egoism, egoism leads to nationalism, and nationalism leads to war';[5] then by former veteran prime minister of Luxembourg and European Commission President designate Jean-Claude Juncker: 'For my generation, the monetary union has always been about forging peace. Today... far too many Europeans are returning to a regional and national mindset... But anyone who believes that the eternal issue of war and peace in Europe has been permanently laid to rest could be making a monumental error. The demons haven't been banished; they are merely sleeping, as the wars in Bosnia and Kosovo have shown us.'[6]. It was to be repeated still more recently by EC President José Manuel Barroso: 'We must never take peace for granted... The European continent has never in its history known such a long period of peace as since the creation of the European Community. It is our duty to preserve and deepen it.'[7]

Aside from preventing renewed military conflict with other member states, many also contend EU membership serves Britain's vital interests for a separate security-related reason. In a rapidly changing post-Cold War world in which the geo-political interests and attention of America are increasingly becoming focused on South America and East Asia, many claim that Britain is liable to find itself increasingly vulnerable to threats to its security emanating from outside Europe unless it remains part of the EU. Some claim that, should Britain leave the EU, it would lose influence with its European partners in NATO, especially France which wants to see the EU replace NATO as Europe's security umbrella. Should that happen, the argument runs, America would be much less willing than it currently is to come to Britain's assistance militarily in the event that its security was ever seriously threatened.

Germany's former defence minister Thomas de Maiziere is one who has advanced this argument. In an interview published by the *Guardian* in April 2013, he stated that: 'If Great Britain leaves the EU... I think from a military point of view the disadvantages for Great Britain would be bigger than the advantages... Outside the EU it would... reduce... [its] influence and this cannot be in the interests of Great Britain. We in Germany would lose a strong partner for a pro-Atlantic cooperation with America... France is not in favour of a stronger role for NATO. The UK is just the opposite.'[8]

Others agree that Britain's security interests are best served through its continued membership of the EU, but for a different reason. They believe that, in the post-Soviet era, NATO has outlived its geo-political purpose, with America no longer having the same incentive to defend Europe. Some go further. They argue that, unless the EU turns itself into a countervailing superpower able to constrain the USA, the future security of EU member states, including Britain, is liable to become increasingly vulnerable to hostile action by third parties responding to unilateral military action undertaken against them by the US carried out in response to perceived threats to its security. Their argument is that, given mounting defence costs plus the nature of the security risks it faces today from non-state actors as well as from other states, Britain needs much closer military integration with its European partners, rather than attempting to go it alone, relying for military assistance on the USA . America may not always be as willing to provide such assistance as she once was, and instead could well become an indirect source of peril to Britain.

Glyn Morgan, Director of the Moynihan European Union Centre at Syracuse University, is someone who has contended that, to enjoy security in the post-Soviet era, EU member states, including Britain, need to become more fully integrated militarily. In support of that contention, Morgan conjures up the following scenario:

> Imagine that, on September 11 next year, terrorists based somewhere in the Maghreb fly hijacked passenger jets into the Westminster parliament, the Reichstag, the Vatican, and the Louvre. These attacks kill thousands. Let it further be imagined that the United States is either preoccupied with China or, in the wake of recent disasters in Iraq, has lost all appetite for foreign military intervention. It is worth bearing this scenario in mind, because given existing military capabilities, Europe's nation-states, acting singly or jointly, would be unable to conduct anything resembling the operation that the United States conducted to destroy Al Qaeda camps in Afghanistan in October and November 2001... It is partly in recognition of Europe's current military weakness and its one-sided dependence on the United States that a number of political leaders have said that Europe needs to become a 'superpower'.[9]

It is not simply to be able to defend themselves more effectively against possible future terrorist attacks, and those willing to harbour terrorist groups, that Morgan argues Britain and other EU member states would enjoy greater security within a militarily integrated EU. By integrating their military capabilities and thereby becoming an independent countervailing super-power, so he argues, a United States of Europe would be able to function as a restraint upon America, and thereby able to deter US military action against third parties who might then be liable to respond in ways inimical to European security.[10]

Morgan's point is that, as it is presently configured, and despite its pretence of being a partnership of equals, the European members of NATO are all still effectively dominated by America. He writes: 'in an age... when the United States not only *is* the world's sole superpower but acts as such – the myth of NATO as an alliance of equals is no longer credible. While eurosceptics are sensitive to the deficits to democratic self-government involved in membership of the EU these deficits are no less pronounced in the case of membership of NATO.'[11] Only by becoming a countervailing super-power of comparable military strength to it, argues Morgan, can European countries, Britain included, hope to contain the security threat otherwise indirectly posed to them by possible unilateral military action undertaken by America. Morgan thus concluded his 2005 book *The Idea of a European Superstate* by observing of Steven Thoburn, the Sunderland greengrocer who challenged the EU's right to decide in what unit measures British retailers had to sell their wares on Britain's high-streets:

The greengrocer who wanted to sell his bananas in imperial measures... demanded... a justification for the very existence of a European level of government... A convincing answer does, however, exist... People like Mr Thoburn... might lament their dependence on political authorities based in Brussels over which they have no control. But th[at] form of dependence... pales into insignificance compared with that a sovereign Britain would face in a world dominated by the United States, China, Russia, and a politically integrated European superstate. The notion that 'independence' could exist outside this European superstate is a mere pipe dream.[12]

Back in 2005, when Morgan published these words, his was something of a lone voice in calling for further

European integration on grounds of security. Over the ensuing decade, he has been joined by several others, including Brendan Simms, professor of the history of international relations at the University of Cambridge, who wrote in 2012:

> As currently configured, the Euro is indeed... a "burning building with no exits"... [However] it cannot be assumed that Europe will be able to reform as a simple free-trading confederation... This will leave Europe rudderless at a time of... massive challenges from outside... [The] tasks facing Europe in the coming decades require the immediate creation of a complete... military union... the creation of a single European army, with the monopoly of external force projection. This is the only structure that will enable Europeans to mobilise in pursuit of their collective destiny.[13]

Clara Marina O'Donnell, a research fellow of the Centre for European Reform, has also recently argued that Britain cannot afford to disengage from the EU's Common Security and Defence Policy (CSDP). Writing in 2011, she contended:

> Since taking office, the coalition partners have shown an unprecedented interest in exploring opportunities for shared defence spending... But... the UK is now interested only in pursuing bilateral cooperation... [T]he predominant trend in UK strategy remains one of disengagement from the CSDP... [B]y leaving EU efforts in a state of 'malign neglect'... the UK is harming its own interests... Britain would be well advised to concern itself less with the threats that might be posed to Britain's independence and the NATO alliance by the emergence of a European army, and more to the risks of a complete loss of European military capability.[14]

A similar argument has been more recently advanced by Sven Biscop, Director of the Europe in the World Programme at the Egmont Royal Institute for International Relations in Brussels. In a 2012 article, he remarked:

> More than ever, it is in the British interest to take a leading role in European defence... As the United States implements its pivot and expects Europeans to act autonomously, Europeans... will increasingly have to deploy on the basis of a collective *European* strategy, based in turn on a collective *European* foreign policy... The UK could continue to block collective European efforts and focus instead on its bilateral cooperation with France... however the combined military power of Britain and France is far from sufficient... France and the UK alone can certainly not afford to acquire all the strategic enablers Europe lacks. To do that requires the critical mass that Europeans collectively can bring... If London abstains or even distances itself from the EU as a whole, an EU-oriented Paris will certainly go ahead anyway... London then really will be left in the cold.[15]

More recently still, Philip Worre, Executive Director of the Brussels-based independent security think-tank ISIS Europe, has claimed that withdrawal from the EU would be contrary to Britain's security interests. Writing in January 2013, Worre argued that: 'A British exit from the EU would have important consequences for the EU, but... Britain would have more to lose... From a security and defence position, by exiting the EU... an isolated Britain would lose considerable power and its standing in world politics.'[16]

Should Britain's security be significantly imperilled by its withdrawing from the EU, that would constitute a very powerful, if not conclusive, reason for its remaining a member, even at the cost of its steadily diminishing sovereignty and independence. The security-based argument for Britain's remaining part of the EU, then, constitutes a substantial part of the political, as against economic, case for its continued membership. To the task of assessing how compelling this argument is, we now turn.

Refutation of the alleged extra security Britain gains from EU membership

The security-based argument for Britain's continued membership of the EU has two strands. One pertains to the security benefits Britain allegedly derives from EU membership *vis-à-vis* other member states, considered either on their own or in consort. The other concerns the security benefits Britain allegedly gains *vis-à-vis* potential threats that emanate from beyond the EU.

Peace and European integration

Are member states of the European Union any less liable to wage war against one another through being members of it? In particular, is Britain less liable to find itself at war with any of them because of being a member of the EU?

Contrary to widespread claims to the contrary, there is no particular reason to suppose that the European Union has served to preserve the peace between member states. While none have fought against each other since its creation, this fact does not establish that it has been responsible for their not having done so. The peace that Europe has enjoyed since the EU was formed no more establishes that the EU was responsible for it than the fact that a particular married couple has enjoyed harmonious relations establishes that this was owing to their marriage. Plenty of marriages end in acrimonious divorce and not all harmonious couples marry.

The EU could have broken up in mutual hostility and violent conflict between member states and it still might.

Meanwhile, several European countries outside the EU have enjoyed just as close and as long-lasting peaceful relations with each other, as they have done with EU member states.

Indeed, history provides plenty of examples of multi-national states that have descended into civil war. The former Yugoslavia is one example; another is present-day Ukraine. Indeed, such a fate seems rather the rule than the exception for states of such a kind. Accordingly, if EU member states have enjoyed peaceful relations with one another since its foundation, it is likely that this stems from another cause. In his 1991 publication *Resisting Leviathan: The Case Against a European State*, Philip Vander Elst put his finger on what has been the probable cause of peace in Europe since 1945:

> The conviction that the existence of the European Community has maintained the peace in Europe since 1957 is extremely naïve. Peace was already an established fact when the EC's founder members signed the Treaty of Rome... Furthermore, the guarantee of this post-war peace was, and still is, the deterrent power of the North Atlantic Alliance, buttressed by the presence of American troops in Europe... The pacifist argument for European Federalism... paradoxically enhances the prospect of future strife, by diverting attention from the real ingredients of political and cultural conflict between nations.... [L]arge international groupings can only operate harmoniously if their member nations are allowed sufficient autonomy to preserve both their separate identity and their capacity for self-determination... [T]hat we are all European nations with a common Christian heritage and democratic institutions... is an insufficient basis on which to build a harmonious and workable federal system.[17]

The cultural and political differences between the peoples of Europe render them too diverse to be able to sustain the kind of pan-European democracy that some, like Jürgen Habermas and more lately Brendan Simms, have hailed as being the panacea for the various ailments that currently beset the EU. Rather than serving as a catalyst of peaceful relations between its members, the EU increasingly seems bent on becoming the cause of mounting tension between member states as their nationals are required to make economic sacrifices on behalf of other member states, whether as their debtors or creditors.

War, peace and nationalism

The suggestion that nationalism is the perennial cause of war, and that cosmopolitan supra-nationalism the sole repository of amity between nations, could not be further from the truth. As the eurosceptic Conservative MEP Daniel Hannan explains in his 2012 book *A Doomed Marriage: Britain and Europe*:

> Looking back over the past half millennium, we find plenty of wars that have ideological rather than national roots... The Thirty Years War (1618–48) was the longest continuous war in Europe's history... yet it divided people by faith not nationality... fascism and communism were to cause far more death and destruction than any nationalist conflicts... Where nationalism *was* at the root of conflict, it was usually nationalism of a people who had been, as it were, incorporated into the wrong state...

> The idea that nationalism is an unstable or dangerous force is, indeed, a remarkably new one. During the Second World War, a constant theme of Churchill's... was that Britain was fighting for the cause of all nations... Again and again, in their war aims and in

their broadcasts to occupied Europe, the Allies stressed that they were fighting to restore the independence of nation-states throughout Europe.[18]

To appreciate how readily nationalistic sentiment can coexist harmoniously alongside universal amity, one need only think of how genuinely fraternal, yet simultaneously nationalistic, are international occasions like the modern Olympic Games. Likewise, as the social psychologist William McDougall noted in his classic 1920 study *The Group Mind*: 'According to the anti-nationalist view, nationalism... is... a kind of disease of human nature... which will have to be sternly repressed and, if possible, eradicated before men can hope to live in peace and tolerable security... [I]ts critics are guilty of the failure to recognise that... it is... capable of infinite variety and of an indefinite degree of intellectualisation and refinement... [and] is not incompatible with still more widely inclusive group sentiments.'[19] Four years later in his 1924 book *Ethics and Some Modern World Problems*, McDougall further elaborated on the ethical value of nationalism:

In spite of all the drawbacks and dangers inevitably involved in the existence of nations and the flourishing of the spirit of nationality... nations are necessary institutions for the following reasons. Man... can be induced to work consistently for the good of his fellow-men, and in harmonious cooperation with them, only by participation in the life of an organised group... [with] a long history in which he may take pride... The universal... or cosmopolitan state cannot replace the nations in... these elevating functions of nationality, for two good reasons. First... men cannot... sympathetically share the desires and emotions, the joys and sorrows of so vast a multitude... Secondly... civilisation as a whole requires, if it is to progress, the variety of social and

political experiment... which can be provided only by...
a number of nations, each developing... its own unique,
historical process.[20]

Kant's Foedus Pacificum and the EU
In the emerging politically centralised European Union,
some have discerned the 'league of peace' (*foedus
pacificum*) which, in his final years, the eighteenth
century German philosopher Immanuel Kant envisaged
would become the nucleus of a global 'ever expanding
federation that [would eventually] prevent war' forever
between nations.[21] However, as has been pointed out by
Simon Glendinning, Director of the LSE-based Forum
for European Philosophy, no greater calumny can be
done Kant than to suppose that the proposed federation
of states on which he placed his hopes for humankind
would be the kind of unitary state that the EU is in the
process of becoming:

> Kant's... basic claim is that impressive constitutional
> improvements seen within... nation states are of limited
> value as long as the destruction of nations through wars
> remains a likely fate. The consolidation of progress... thus
> calls for a 'general agreement between nations'... Some
> of Kant's remarks suggest... that what Kant is proposing
> is... a new supra-national governing body arising first
> in the form of a united European state and thence in
> the 'final step' in a united world state. [But] Kant never
> loses sight of the fact that in an international context
> one is always faced with relations between *singular
> sovereign wills*... and [that] the voluntary formation of a
> 'great political body' *by nations* can only bring into being
> a relatively stable 'united will' not... a new singular
> 'general will'... He also thinks that an international state
> is likely to be too big to administer in a non-despotic

way... For Kant... the lawless state of nature and the condition of 'universal despotism in an international state'... are to be avoided, and so Kant calls instead for... a form of federation... [that] does not aim to acquire any power like that of a state, but merely to preserve and secure the freedom of each state... If we want to avoid the two graveyards of freedom for Europe today we should follow him.[22]

Elsewhere, Glendinning points out that: '[It] may well be... that euroscepticism is on the rise across Europe. But... eurofederalism is not the only alternative for Europe: a voluntary league of nations remains... our greatest opportunity for making war in Europe less likely and allowing "our part of the world" to flourish.'[23] Glendinning entitled the article from which this last quotation was taken: 'Europe should reject Jürgen Habermas' vision of a federal European state and instead create an enduring association between sovereign nations.' The only point where issue might be taken with Glendinning is the implicit suggestion that some further action is needed by Europe to bring such an association into being. There is no need, for such an association already exists in the form of NATO which, as well as including most European countries, also includes the USA, Canada and Turkey.

As we have seen, however, some have questioned whether NATO can any longer serve a useful purpose in the present post-communist age. Some have also claimed that, unless European countries break free of American hegemony and establish their own autonomous security arrangements, they will remain in thrall to the USA and hence vulnerable to blow-back from any unilateral military action that it might undertake against third parties. Should that be so, and should acquisition of an autonomous defence capability require EU member states to integrate their military forces, it would seem that Britain might need to remain within the EU, even at the eventual cost of having to cede control of its military forces. This takes us to the second strand of the security case for Britain's continued membership of the EU.

NATO, the USA and European security
As we have seen, those who today call for EU member states to pool their defence capabilities and to integrate them more deeply rest their case on one or both of the following two claims. The first claim is that, in the post-Cold War era, NATO no longer serves any real strategic purpose and so EU member states must collectively assume the burden of looking after their own security. The second claim is that, only by combining to form an autonomous military superpower can any of these states, including Britain, hope to enjoy as much security as they derive from their current military alliance with America, but minus the security risks that attend that alliance. A corollary of both claims is that Britain's security is best served by its remaining within the EU and by its assisting the EU to become a military superpower through integrating its own military capabilities with those of other member states. How valid are these two claims?

As regards the first, there is reason to reject its underlying assumption that NATO has outlived its purpose and value. As was once famously remarked of NATO by its first Secretary, General Lord Hastings Ismay, its original purpose was 'to keep the Americans in, the Russians out, and the Germans down'. Since the collapse of the Soviet Union, Europe has faced little threat of Russian invasion.

Likewise, since 1945, Germany has been as averse to hard power as it was previously keen on it. As to America, since it was only present in Europe militarily to keep the Russians out and the Germans down, it can seem there is no longer any need for its military presence there or indeed for NATO itself. However, such appearances are deceptive. As was observed in 2006 by Julian Lindley-French, Senior Fellow of the Institute of Statecraft and formerly Eisenhower Professor of Defence Strategy at the Netherlands Defence Academy:

> Far from being a hangover from cold war days... the Atlantic alliance will remain essential to the strategies of both Europe and the United States... With the collapse of the always fragile strategic consensus with Russia and China, it is difficult for Washington to be sure that its action will ever be 'legalised' through the UN... in all but the most extreme situations... NATO is... part of a new transatlantic contract in which Europeans minimise the very considerable risk their forces face in the field [in mainly humanitarian missions] and, in return, they legitimise American-led structural interventions... when Europeans so agree.[24]

Subsequent events seem to have confirmed Lindley-French's contention, for reasons which have been noted by Olivier Schmitt, an associate researcher with the French Strategic Research Institute École Militaire, who writes:

> The relations between NATO and the EU have been the subject of countless articles, conferences and reports. After a decade of debates on the proper scope and focus of both institutions, the hard truth remains: NATO means the United States which means military capabilities and reassurance incommensurate with what any aggregation of European states could generate. If security means territorial defence, then NATO is European security.[25]

Schmitt points to the striking fact that, since: 'the negative results of the French and Dutch referenda on the European constitution in 2005... almost all of the main institutional initiatives that are now showcased by optimists as proof of European successes were in fact launched before 2005... [T]he military committee, the European Defence Agency, the battle-groups, and so on were all created or conceptualised before the 2005 political crisis. After that, nothing really important happened.'[26]

Europe continues to depend on NATO for its security, but so does America, according to Luke Coffey, Margaret Thatcher Fellow at the Heritage Foundation and before that a special senior advisor on defence and security matters to former UK Defence Secretary Liam Fox. In an article published by the Heritage Foundation in May 2013, Coffey writes:

The commonly held belief that US forces are in Europe to protect European allies from a threat that no longer exists is wrong ... [B]asing American troops in Europe is first and foremost in the US national security interest. It is true that the presence of US forces in Europe contributes to the collective defence of European allies, but this is a consequence of, not the reason for, maintaining a robust military presence... One of the most obvious benefits of having US troops in Europe is its geographical proximity to some of the most dangerous and contested regions in the world – Russia, the Arctic, Iran, Asia Minor, the Caspian Sea and North Africa... The US has unique security interests around the European region that require a robust US force presence regardless of Europe's military capabilities... The US military presence in Europe deters American [sic] adversaries, strengthens allies, and protects American interests. The basing and support cost of the almost 50,000 US troops in Germany cost... last year... less than one per cent of the overall [US] defence budget.[27]

Assuming that Coffey is correct, the Americans will not be disengaging militarily from Europe for the foreseeable future. Were Europe or its energy supply lines ever to be threatened with attack, there is no reason to suppose that it would lack rapid military assistance from the USA. As a result, there seems little reason for the EU to seek to develop an autonomous military capability outside of NATO. Whether Britain would wish to be part of such a development can depend only on whether, in the final analysis, European military independence from America would constitute any strategic benefit to Britain. Glyn Morgan, as we have seen, contends that the EU needs to turn itself into an autonomous military superpower so as to be able to deter America from unilateral military action against third parties that might provoke retaliation against Europe. Certainly, so long as Britain remains allied to an America that is engaged in mortal combat with Al Qaeda, it will be more exposed to such risk than it would be as part of a more militarily neutral Europe. This consideration takes us to the second security-based argument in support of Britain's continued membership of the EU: that Britain would enjoy greater security as part of an EU that had turned itself into an autonomous military superpower than it would do outside of the EU.

There are several reasons why serious issue might be taken with the foregoing argument. In the first place, it assumes that only a superpower of comparable military stature to America is capable of exerting sufficient restraint on it to be able to induce it to desist from what its allies might perceive to be unduly rash or unwise unilateral military action. Such an assumption underestimates the influence that Britain still continues to be able to exert on America despite its having nothing like as much military power. That influence was clearly on display in the effect that the Westminster parliamentary vote of August 2013 against military action in Syria had on America, which quickly followed suit in calling off its planned military action against the Syrian regime, despite continued French support for such action. Notwithstanding claims made at the time of this parliamentary vote that it signalled the end of Britain's 'special relationship' with America, the two countries remain the closest of allies. America needs Britain's moral, if not always logistical, support for any proposed military venture on which it might wish to embark to legitimise it in the court of world opinion. Shortly after the Westminster vote, James Rogers, international relations lecturer at the Baltic Defence College in Tartu, Estonia, astutely remarked that:

> [A]s Washington pivots and entrenches in the Far East, the United States will continue to need the United Kingdom – perhaps even more than it did during the Cold War... The United Kingdom does not, and never has, simply danced to an American tune. Further, the United States is not a unilateral titan that can do whatever it likes: it is constrained – by the British...the two countries are heavily co-dependent... to provide the sanction and legitimacy the other needs to act.[28]

There is, therefore, no reason to suppose that, should Britain withdraw from the EU, it would enjoy any less influence with America than it already has. Indeed, there is reason to suppose that Britain might well acquire much greater influence with America. This is because, without Britain as a member, the EU is likely to become increasingly detached from the USA strategically, and the USA increasingly reliant upon Britain for a strategic presence within Europe.

Second, the notion that Britain would enjoy more security within a militarily integrated autonomous EU than it would do outside the EU in military alliance with America overestimates the extent to which the terror threat that Britain faces today from violent Islamist extremism is caused by its alliance with America rather than by other factors that would still render it a target of such terror. The likes of al-Qaeda still harbour plenty of other grievances against the non-Muslim world that would leave Britain a legitimate target of terror in their eyes. Consider by way of illustration the following communiqué issued in March 2006 by Ayman al-Zawahiri, the leader of al-Qaeda since the demise of Osama bin Laden:

> In France, a Muslim father cannot prevent his daughter from having sex, because she is protected by the law, but this same law punishes her if she covers her hair... And in England, they punish those who encourage terrorism yet no one dares to punish those who... insult our prophet... [W]e cannot fight these insults by demonstrations and burning embassies alone... [W]e need to rise as one nation [and] fight [with] ... everything that we have... [W]e have to ask ourselves: are we ready to sacrifice ourselves... If we are... we need to... inflict losses on the western crusader, especially to its economic infrastructure with strikes that would make it bleed for years. The strikes on New York, Washington, Madrid and London are the best examples.[29]

Whether Britain likes it or not, it currently faces a serious terror threat from violent Islamist extremism that would certainly survive its military detachment from America. So does the rest of Europe.

In July 2013 at the annual National Security Conference in London, the Director of the Office for Security and Counter-terrorism Charles Farr warned that: 'there are more people associated with al-Qaeda and al-Qaeda associated organisations now operating in Syria than there have ever been before... They are much closer to us, in much greater numbers and fighting with an intensity that we have not seen before... Groups in Syria aspire to attack Europe and have the capability and means to do so, including returning foreign fighters coming back to Britain... I think it is the most profound shift in the threat we have seen... since 2003.'[30]

How and why EU membership is imperilling Britain's external security

Given the very real threat of terror from violent Islamist extremism that Britain continues to face, there can be little doubt that its security is enhanced, rather than diminished, by its continuing alliance with America. Their resultant pooling of intelligence has enabled each of them to defuse several terror plots. Arguably, given the enhanced security that its alliance with America provides for Britain, should it ever have to choose between America or EU membership, its security would be better served by continuing its alliance with America than by remaining an EU member.

However, these alternatives by no means exhaust the possibilities open to Britain. As things stand, at least on the surface, Britain seems perfectly able to enjoy the best of both worlds, by remaining allied with America through NATO while also a member of the EU. On the surface at least, therefore, continuation of the status quo might seem Britain's best strategic option. However, that surface impression is an illusion because the status quo is becoming increasingly less stable. In practice, Britain's security is becoming ever more compromised by its continued membership of an EU that is beginning to become more integrated militarily.

There are several reasons why Britain's external security would be better served by its withdrawing from the EU and pursuing its defence collaboration with other European states only through NATO or else on a bilateral basis than by remaining a member. First, the more integrated the military capabilities of EU member states and their defence industries become, the more reliant are they for their security on the EU and the less able to deploy military force unilaterally. Any greater reliance on the EU could well jeopardise Britain's security because, apart from France and a couple of other member states, Britain's EU partners have consistently shown themselves to be less willing to expend public money on defence, as the following statistics show:

> EU nations have a combined gross domestic product (GDP) of... some 124 per cent of the US total. However, the combined 2009 defence budgets of the EU totalled €188bn compared with the 2009 US defence budget of €503bn.The EU member states thus spend some 35 per cent of the US expenditure on defence... Between 2001 and 2008 EU member states' spending on defence fell from €255 billion to €223 billion... Furthermore, of that [2009] €188bn France and the UK together represent 43 per cent... while France, Germany and the UK represent 61 per cent... [O]ver the roughly same period the US increased its defence expenditure by 109 per cent, China by 247 per cent, Russia by 67 per cent and Australia by 56 per cent.[31]

Similarly, aside from France and a couple of other member states, Britain's EU partners have consistently displayed equal reluctance to place their military in harm's way in situations that, in the judgment of both America and Britain, have warranted military deployment. In his valedictory address in February 2010, former US Defence Secretary Robert Gates warned about the detrimental effects that such reluctance on the part of Britain's EU partners is having on the security of members of NATO. He said: 'The demilitarisation of Europe – where large swathes of the general public and political class are averse to military force and the risks that go with it – has gone from a blessing in the twentieth century to an impediment to achieving real security and lasting peace in the twenty-first… real or perceived weakness [can] be a temptation to miscalculation and aggression.'[32] The potentially adverse effects on Britain's security of the unwillingness of its EU partners to deploy force can be gauged from what was said about the matter by the Centre for European Reform in its submission to the Government's Balance of Competences Review. It stated that:

> Many European countries are even more averse to incur the costs and risks of conflict when deploying under the EU flag than when deploying under NATO. As a result, a number of CSDP missions have been too short, too small or too cautious to make a lasting impact on the ground. For example, the EU only has about 60 officials advising Iraqis on how to improve their judiciary and policing. For several years, EU countries had only around 200 police officers training police forces in Afghanistan. And European governments placed so many safety restrictions on their police officers that their ability to help Afghan forces was curtailed.[33]

Germany is among the most reluctant of EU member states to deploy military forces in combat situations. Its reluctance has already had adverse effects on the effectiveness of military operations of its other EU partners. A case in point was the 2011 NATO operation that Britain and France undertook against the regime of Colonel Gaddafi in Libya. As former US Undersecretary of State Nicholas Burns remarked: 'There's no question that the European members of NATO would have been more effective as a military unit if German forces had contributed to the mission.'[34] Likewise, Tom Dyson, a lecturer in international relations at Royal Holloway College, has stated that: 'By opposing military action in Libya, Germany ensured that the CSDP could not be used as a framework for action, thereby undermining its effectiveness and credibility.'[35]

The reluctance of so many EU member states to deploy military force bodes ill for Britain, especially if EU defence integration means that Britain will increasingly have to look to the EU for security rather than depend on its own capabilities or those of America. Compare the reaction of Britain's EU partners with that of America to the seizure by the Iranian navy in 2007 of 15 Royal Naval personnel whilst on patrol in the Gulf: 'While Britain's European neighbours... refused to specify any retaliatory measures in support of a fellow EU member, the United States gave Britain an unequivocal demonstration of its support, conducting its largest naval exercise in the Gulf since 2003. Through its deployment of aircraft and warships, America effectively gave Britain a security guarantee that it would stand shoulder-to-shoulder at any cost during this major international incident.'[36]

There is a second reason why Britain's external security is likely to be better served by its withdrawal from the EU than by its continued EU membership. The more militarily integrated do EU member states become, the weaker and less effective NATO is left. This is because of the deep reluctance of so many EU member states to support and deploy military force. As a result, such military assets as member states do make available to the EU come via a process known as 'double-hatting' whereby their being made available to the EU comes at the expense of their availability to NATO. The reasons why have been cogently set out by Luke Coffey:

Proponents of EU defence integration argue that military capabilities developed under the auspices of the CSDP will always be made available to NATO... if, and when, NATO was ever to request the[m]... This may sound good in theory but is unlikely to work in practice... Any time that EU military assets are used, unanimous agreement by all EU members is required. Six veto-wielding EU members are not members of NATO. Of these six countries, five are established neutral countries: Ireland, Austria, Malta, Sweden, and Finland. The other, Cyprus, is politically hostile toward NATO member Turkey and has a track record of blocking NATO-EU cooperation in the past.[37]

There are two further reasons why EU defence integration is liable to progressively weaken NATO. First, EU defence integration must inexorably lead to unnecessary and wasteful duplication of military forces and assets. A perfect illustration of this is provided by the proposed EU operational headquarters, currently much canvassed by supporters of EU defence integration. As Luke Coffey has noted of the proposal: 'The EU already has access to the full range of NATO's military headquarters at SHAPE (Supreme Headquarters Allied Powers Europe)... Furthermore, the EU has access to five national military headquarters for use for EU-led missions. The estimated cost of establishing an EU military operational headquarters is tens of millions of dollars.'[38]

Second, EU defence integration must inexorably decouple EU military forces and assets from those that belong to NATO's non-EU members, most notably, to America, thereby reducing their mutual interoperability. EU defence integration must, therefore, inevitably reduce the capacity of British forces to operate in the field alongside those of one of its oldest allies for the sake of their becoming better able to operate alongside those of countries which have been far less willing than America has been to deploy force on behalf of Britain.

This decoupling of American and European forces is already occurring through the diverging procurement policies that are being adopted by the EU in the name of defence integration. Britain is, thus, steadily becoming ever more firmly locked into military partnership with other EU member states while simultaneously locked out of potential future military partnership with America. As Lee Rotherham, an adviser to three successive shadow foreign secretaries, has observed of these trends:

> NATO… has led to a measure of harmonisation… [This] makes sense [since]… if you can't radio the Americans you can't ask them to bomb the right hill… EU military integration, however, is… different… [Being] driven by political aspirations… [its] inevitable end direction is an integrated military… rather than the strategic interests of any individual member states… It… risk[s] our genuinely privileged access to the Pentagon and to the US defence procurement establishment… The UK is currently signed up to the EU's Defence Agency. Ostensibly… a harmless and commonsensical tool for getting (supposedly) cheap procurement… its track record… demonstrates… it is an instrument of military integration… to rationalise defence industries, with capability being shut down and divvied across the EU.[39]

As has been noted by Richard North, EU defence integration is currently placing Britain in an acute strategic dilemma: 'the crucial question for the UK… is whether it goes for European or US cooperation… [It] can no longer act in… [its] traditional role as a bridge between the two.'[40] For all who are more concerned with Britain's future security than with EU integration, it is clear how Britain should choose in the face of this dilemma. As has been wisely remarked: 'It is an illusion to think that NATO and a European Army could co-exist in an effective fashion. The end result would be a weak-kneed and feckless EU defence force... [that] would sound the death knell of NATO... splitting the alliance in half, and ultimately weakening transatlantic defence... Great Britain should firmly oppose it and refuse any cooperation with the development of an independent EU defence identity.'[41]

There is one further reason why Britain's security is more likely to be enhanced rather than diminished by its withdrawing from the EU. It stems from the consistent unwillingness shown by so many with any political power in the EU towards cooperation with America's counter-terrorism efforts. A case in point is the unwillingness of so many within the EU Parliament to accord the US Treasury's Terrorist Finance Tracking Programme (TFTP) access to financial data held electronically by the Belgium-based international banking syndicate, the Society for Worldwide Interbank Financial Telecommunications, known by its acronym SWIFT.

Ever since 9/11 2001, SWIFT has granted the TFTP access to its data. Until the start of 2010, some of the SWIFT servers that held the data were located in the USA. Hence the TFTP could freely access SWIFT data without the permission of European governments. After all of the SWIFT servers were relocated to Europe at the end of 2009, the US authorities needed the agreement of both the European Commission and European Parliament to access the data, under the terms of the Lisbon Treaty. One of the very first acts of the European Parliament upon acquiring its new powers was to vote in February 2010 to deny the TFTP access to the SWIFT data. This vote was not rescinded until June of that year after the European Commission had reached a new agreement with Washington on what data the TFTP could access.

Following publication in May 2013 of disclosures by former NSA employee Edward Snowden about American counter-terrorism intelligence gathering in Europe, strong opposition has once again manifested itself in the European Parliament towards EU cooperation with America in connection with SWIFT. Former Belgian Prime Minister and MEP Guy Verhofstadt has said: 'If there is the slightest doubt that the US authorities are in breach, the Commission should immediately initiate to suspend the agreement pending clarifications.'[42]

The EU's current agreement with the US over access to SWIFT is due for renewal in 2015 and can be terminated by a qualified majority vote by heads of government of EU member states. Should America be denied access to SWIFT, Britain's security is liable to be seriously compromised, as can be seen from the following statement by the US Treasury Department about the effectiveness of the TFTP:

> Since its inception in 2001, the TFTP has provided valuable lead information and has aided in the prevention of many terrorist attacks and in the investigation of many of the most visible and violent terrorist attacks and attempted attacks of the past decade... A significant number of the leads generated by the TFTP have been shared with EU Member State Governments, with more than 1,800 such reports through July 2011... [A]n independent person appointed by the EU conducted two reviews of the TFTP... [reporting] in 2008 and in early 2010... that TFTP leads shared with EU authorities had not only been extremely valuable in investigating attacks which have taken place in Europe over the last eight years, but had also been instrumental in *preventing* a number of terrorist attacks in Europe and elsewhere.[43]

The additional internal security EU membership allegedly brings Britain

So far, our discussion of the impact Britain's membership of the EU is having on its security has largely been focused on what can be called Britain's *external security*. By this expression is meant its degree of invulnerability to acts of aggression by foreign powers or by other non-state foreign actors such as international terrorist organisations like Al Qaeda. There remains for consideration the impact that Britain's EU membership is having, or is in the future liable to have, on what can be termed Britain's *internal security*. By this expression is meant the degree of invulnerability that its nationals enjoy against acts of aggression by other nationals, including, most notably, by officials of the state, such as for example the police, while acting in an official capacity.

A country whose nationals could at any time be indefinitely detained without trial by the authorities would enjoy little by way of internal security. They would do so, no matter how safe they were rendered by this practice from foreign aggression, civil unrest and crime. To minimise how much coercion state officials can lawfully use while acting in an official capacity, most countries place strict legal constraints upon them by means of bills of rights and other legal instruments.

As in the case of external security, the EU initially deemed all matters relating to what here is being termed the internal security of member states outside its purview. Over the last quarter of a century, however, the EU has increasingly begun to concern itself with matters relating to the internal security of its member states. This change has largely come about as a result of the freedom of movement that the EU accords their nationals to travel, reside, and work anywhere within it. As the EU has been among the first to recognise, such freedom of movement has considerably increased the scope within the EU for cross-border organised crime, such as drug-trafficking and people-trafficking.

The EU has created various agencies and legal instruments to facilitate cooperation between member states in matters relating to criminal law enforcement. These agencies and instruments include: Europol, Eurojust, SIRENE and CEPOL. Europol is the EU's law enforcement agency with almost 800 staff at its headquarters in the Hague. Eurojust is the EU's self-styled 'Judicial Cooperation Unit'. It is also based in the Hague. SIRENE, whose full title is 'Supplementary Information Request at the National Entry', is an information-pooling association of states within the Schengen area. It has bureaus in all countries within that area. CEPOL is the European Police College based in Bramshill, Hampshire. Its function is to bring together senior police officers from across the EU for the purpose of their networking and developing cross-border cooperation. Most notoriously of all, among the arrangements for closer integration between EU member states in matters relating to criminal law enforcement is the European Arrest Warrant (EAW). The arrangement came into force in 2004 to expedite the extradition of criminal suspects between EU member states.

All of these various developments are liable to have a profound and potentially detrimental impact on the quality of policing and law enforcement in Britain to the extent that it becomes a party to them. At the time of the Lisbon Treaty, Britain secured a potentially indefinite opt-out from 135 legal measures in the area of freedom, security and justice that the EU had adopted before December 2009, when that treaty was due to come into effect. The measures from which Britain gained this opt-out included the European Arrest Warrant. By 1 June 2014, however, the UK government must notify the EU into which of these measures it wishes to opt as from 1 December 2014, and which of them it wishes to continue to opt out of. All such measures as it decides to adopt will from then on cease to fall within the exclusive jurisdiction of the UK. Instead, from then on they will be determined at EU level at which the UK lacks veto power. In the case of the legal measures out of which it chooses to continue to opt, Britain can always seek their suitable amendment before applying to opt into them. Once adopted, however, they too will cease to be matters over which it would any longer enjoy sovereignty.

Britain is thus faced with a momentous decision about some of the most sensitive matters relating to internal security. In July 2013, the British government announced its intention to opt out of all 135 measures, save for 35 of them into which it declared that it would be prepared to opt, provided that beforehand it could obtain their suitable amendment. One of these measures that into which the government indicated itself willing to opt was a suitably amended version of the EAW in a form as yet to be agreed.

Advocates of EU integration and of its close involvement in the area of freedom, security and justice claim that the internal security of member states has been considerably enhanced by the EU's various legal agencies and instruments. Underlying its ever-increasing involvement in policing and criminal justice is its presumption that the police services and criminal justice systems of its member states warrant, or at least can all readily be made to warrant, their mutual recognition, in the sense of being judged as being of equal probity.

Whilst there is an unanswerable case for Britain's close cooperation with other EU countries in matters concerning policing and criminal justice, there is no less strong a case for doubting that the police forces and criminal justice systems of all other member states have anything like as much probity as do Britain's, for all their imperfections. Among the oldest and most cherished legal instrument in Britain for safeguarding the civil rights and liberties of its nationals is their right to trial before a lay jury in cases of serious alleged crime. Other safeguards include *habeas corpus*, that is the right to a swift hearing of charges in open court before incarceration and a relatively speedy trial (within six months) once charges have been formally brought.

Comparable legal safeguards are lacking in many other EU member states. The main grounds for misgiving in this connection were well formulated by the House of Commons Home Affairs Select Committee in its October 2013 report on the 35 pre-Lisbon EU police and criminal justice measures into which the government has announced itself minded to opt: 'The European Arrest Warrant... in its existing form... is fundamentally flawed. It is based on a system of mutual recognition of legal systems, which in reality vary significantly. Some countries may seek extradition simply to expedite their investigations whereas others do so in pursuit of relatively minor crimes... Furthermore, the EAW is based on a flawed assumption of mutual trust in the standards of justice of other member states. As such, it has facilitated miscarriages of justice in a number of cases, irrevocably damaging the lives of those affected.'[44] As Lord (Norman) Lamont warned in a speech about the EAW:

Clearly the concept of the presumption of innocence means different things in Britain from other European countries. To the British mind, the idea of the investigating magistrate detaining someone for an indefinite period without charge simply for the purpose of investigation is at odds with the presumption of innocence; indeed, many people would call it outrageous. It is not so in continental countries. The practice of the investigating magistrate has been accepted under the European Convention on Human Rights as consistent with the presumption of innocence. In Germany, France, Italy, Spain or Belgium, an investigating magistrate can hold someone without charge for questioning for quite long periods. Pressure thus builds on the detained person to strike a bargain with the prosecuting authority and concede guilt.[45]

There are, therefore, very substantial reasons why Britain should exercise the utmost caution before ceding to the EU any sovereignty over policing and criminal justice. It is not xenophobia or misplaced jingoism that counsels such caution, but palpable fact.

The true diminution in internal security that Britain suffers by EU membership

Despite claims to the contrary, the laws and policies adopted by the EU to turn itself into 'an area of freedom, security and justice' have made Britain a less free, less secure and less just country. In February 2014, the Home Office published a dossier of 'Evidence of Fraud and Abuse of Free Movement in the UK' that had been submitted to the EC the previous December in advance of a meeting of the EU Home Affairs Council.[46] The dossier detailed the scale and organised nature of the abuse, most notably people-trafficking from the EU into Britain by organised gangs for subsequent criminal purposes, such as organised begging, benefit fraud, and sham marriages with non-EU nationals who seek thereby to evade deportation from Britain.

The dossier mentioned one case in which: 'over 1,000 children had been trafficked by a Romanian gang from the town of Tanderai for the purpose of exploitation through forced criminality, including theft, organised begging and benefit fraud.' In another instance, the dossier reported: 'A Poland-based gang had lured at least 230 Polish victims, many of whom had mental health or substance abuse problems, to come to the UK by promising them work. Instead, the victims were tricked into opening bank accounts, into which fraudulently-claimed benefits would be paid. The money would subsequently be emptied from the accounts by the gang, leaving the victims destitute.'

The lives and security of ordinary British citizens and of others who legitimately reside in Britain have been adversely affected by the freedom of movement that the EU has been so keen to see extended to nationals of its member states. A case in point arises from the recent large influx into Britain of Roma beggars. Their arrival has been accompanied by a sharp rise in petty crime in those parts of central London to which they have tended to gravitate on account of their high concentrations of wealthy Arab residents who are widely known to consider it their religious duty to give alms to whoever should seek them. Although the British authorities have made great efforts at the taxpayers' expense to repatriate these Roma beggars, their efforts to date have met with little success. As was reported by the British press in late September 2013:

> [T]he Roma of Park Lane have boomeranged back... Their return... highlights... the difficulty of policing what are effectively Britain's open borders – and the burden put on the state by Europe's freedom-of-movement rules... Under European law, the Romanians have a right to be here for 90 days. After that, they need to be working, studying or self-sufficient. Sleeping rough and begging are grounds for removal. By offering to pay for travel home the Government is avoiding a potentially expensive legal battle, which can only begin once the 90-day limit has been passed... [F]or the Roma of Park Lane, sleeping rough is a more rewarding prospect than what awaits at home.[47]

Petty crime committed by Roma has by no means been confined to Britain or its capital city. In April 2013, staff at Paris's Louvre museum walked out in protest at the high rates of petty theft being carried out there by organised groups of Roma children. One staff member said: 'The children are tough and very well organised. They stop at nothing to get what they want, and work in gangs. We can only do so much, but arrests are usually impossible because of their young age. If they are kicked out, they return the next day. They are very aggressive towards staff...'[48] In 2011, the then French Interior minister was reported as having claimed that the vast majority of street robberies in Paris were carried out by children of Romanian immigrants.

Similarly, in a radio interview in November 2013, former Labour Home Secretary David Blunkett expressed concern about the scale of anti-social behaviour on the party of the fast growing Roma community in the Page Hall area of Sheffield. He said: 'We have got to change the behaviour and the culture of the incoming community, the Roma community, because there's going to be an explosion otherwise. We all know that... We've got to be tough and robust in saying to people you are not in a downtrodden village or woodland, because many of them don't even live in areas where there are toilets or refuse collection facilities. You are not there anymore, you are here – and you've got to adhere to our standards, and to our way of behaving...'[49]

Outbreaks of petty crime by Roma point to a larger, more general threat to the internal security of member states that freedom of movement within the EU for their nationals has created. It has made it much more difficult for each of them to control its borders.

The European Arrest Warrant
Before the introduction of the European Arrest Warrant in 2004, British courts were able to exercise some oversight over extradition requests by other EU member states to ensure that there was a *prima facie* case against

whoever's extradition was being sought and that the charges against them were sufficiently grave to warrant extradition. Since the introduction of the EAW, Britain's criminal justice system has been unable to do anything but comply with such warrants, provided the relevant forms have been completed correctly. Despite all claims to the contrary, there are few other EU member states whose criminal justice systems share the same level of concern as that of the United Kingdom to ensure that none of its nationals are deprived of liberty without adequate cause and due process. Britain's centuries-old common law traditions of *habeas corpus*, trial by jury and the presumption of innocence are not necessarily to be found in all other EU member states.

Cases are now legion of British citizens having been arrested in Britain on European Arrest Warrants and then sent abroad for incarceration without trial, sometimes for lengthy periods, often on the merest suspicion or for quite trivial offences that in Britain would not be considered to merit a custodial sentence. When eventually brought to trial, those arrested on such warrants have undergone trial not, as in Britain, before a jury of peers, but rather by juries led by professional magistrates, which increases the likelihood of conviction irrespective of their innocence or guilt. As was remarked by Conservative MP Dominic Raab: 'The European Arrest Warrant lacks the most basic safeguards that would allow judicial scrutiny to protect British citizens from such manifest miscarriages of justice.'[50]

Three notable cases of such injustice are those of Andrew Symeou, Garry Mann and Michael Turner.[51] In 2009, Andrew Symeou was extradited from Britain to Greece on an EAW. He was there kept incarcerated in appalling conditions for nearly a year, before being bailed and eventually cleared of manslaughter charges that had been based on witness statements that Greek police had obtained through violent intimidation and which were later retracted.

Garry Mann was a former fireman from Kent who, in 2004, was arrested in Portugal and summarily tried, convicted and sentenced to a two year prison sentence, all within 48 hours of arrest, for alleged offences connected with a football riot during the Euro football tournament hosted by Portugal that year. After being told that he need not serve his sentence should he agree to being deported and not to return to Portugal for a year, Mann was subsequently arrested in Britain on an EAW in 2009 and returned to Portugal where he was made to serve a year of his sentence. This was after an English court had in 2005 decided that Mann had been denied a fair trial in Portugal, when it refused to grant an application by British police for a worldwide football banning order against Mann.

Michael Turner is a Dorset businessman who, in November 2012, was, along with a business partner, convicted of fraud and sentenced to a five month prison sentence, suspended for two years. Their charges and convictions arose as a result of the collapse in 2005 of a time-share company of theirs in Hungary that allegedly had left creditors there owed £18,000.[52] In 2009, Turner was extradited to Hungary from Britain on an EAW. He was held there for four months under very arduous conditions before being released and allowed to return to Britain, pending further police investigations. During his incarceration in Hungary, Turner was interviewed by police only once. Although EAWs are supposedly to be issued only for the arrest of those who have been convicted or are in the process of being prosecuted, Turner's extradition occurred before Hungarian police had decided whether to prosecute him.

Unless the British government decides to opt out of this legal measure, or else manages to secure its radical revision, Britain will soon be relinquishing centuries-old legal safeguards designed to prevent miscarriages of justice for the sake of little discernible benefit in terms of its internal security. As the current Lord Chief Justice of England and Wales Baron Thomas of Cwmgiedd candidly remarked concerning the system of European Arrest Warrants in oral evidence to the 2011 Scott Baker enquiry about Britain's extradition arrangements with other countries: 'There is quite a lot of strong judicial feeling... in northern Europe that both the judges and politicians in other countries [within the EU] need to put the resources into their systems to bring them up to standard.'[53]

While there is need for robust extradition arrangements between Britain and other EU member states, it is quite wrong to suggest that, in its present form, the European Arrest Warrant has done anything but diminish the internal security Britain and the British have traditionally enjoyed. Even if, as the British government hopes, it were to succeed in eliminating the worst excesses of the system of these arrest warrants, there seems little reason why extradition should fall under the purview of the EU at all. While extradition between EU member states might take longer without an EAW, the chances of miscarriages of justice against any British nationals would then be very much lower, a cost surely worth bearing.

The ultimate political cost to Britain of EU membership: surrender of parliamentary sovereignty and political freedom

Once Britain hands over any judicial powers to the EU such as terms of extradition, then the Westminster parliament loses control over them as long as Britain remains an EU member. Indeed, it is part of EU jurisprudence that, once any directive or regulation has been incorporated into EU law, it is not to be rescinded. The unwillingness of the

EU to rescind any part of its body of law marks a huge difference in political culture between virtually all other member states and Britain which has always accorded its parliament complete sovereignty in the sense of being able to unmake any laws that have been made there. The consequence of this parliamentary sovereignty has been to ensure that the British people have ultimately retained sovereignty, since it is they who decide who their legislators are. Hence, any unpopular laws can be reversed by fresh parliamentary representatives.

This element of reversibility and accountability is wholly missing from the EU. It is this lack that constitutes the true democratic deficit from which it is widely acknowledged to suffer. No one saw more clearly than the historian Arthur Bryant what great a loss of political freedom the British people would suffer by entering the EU. Writing in 1962, at the time of Britain's first application to join, he observed:

> Whatever the economic advantages of the Common Market, they cannot outweigh the immense advantages, or rather lack of disadvantages, that we have derived in the past and can still derive in the future from our conducting our political affairs in such a way as to avoid... laying down rules for... posterity so rigid that they cannot be changed without revolution. With the exception of the phlegmatic Dutch and the numerically insignificant Luxemburgers, all our proposed partners in the Common Market have suffered from repeated revolutions, some of them of a most violent and bloody kind... None of these upheavals and all the misery and bloodshed, not to mention economic dislocation and even ruin caused by them, would have taken place had the rulers, and by implication the peoples, of these countries not insisted on binding, not merely themselves, but their successors and so denying to posterity the wherewithal

to accept and register necessary change... For whatever may be said for or against the very able and deeply sincere makers of the Common Market, rigidity of rule is the essence of their planning and, in their eyes, an indispensable and necessary virtue.[54]

Even if the EU were to institute European-wide elections and acquire a directly elected president who was able, along with the EU Parliament, to rescind as well as to enact European laws, the EU would still suffer from a major democratic deficit from which Britain has long been spared. Or at least used to be spared. For, in a very real sense, the Westminster Parliament no longer enjoys full sovereignty as long as Britain remains an EU member. The diversity of EU member states means that there is no European *demos*. Without one, there can never be a sufficiently united body of public opinion within the EU as would enable its peoples to identify with those who make European law as well as with one another. Without both such forms of identification, the laws enacted in Brussels will always lack democratic legitimacy, despite the ritual of EU elections.

The absence of a genuine European *demos* means that the nationals of EU member states will always remain alienated and disengaged from whoever is elected to the EU Parliament, as they also will be from the laws made there save insofar as they are affected by them personally, or, at best, nationally. In such circumstances, EU politics will inevitably become a charade of coalitions and competing interest groups without any real concern for the good of the whole. The result will be the emergence of a growing divide between the ever more politically alienated peoples of Europe and a governing elite of professional politicians and administrators who will not hesitate to accrue more and more power and privileges. Meanwhile, Europe's peoples will become increasingly disengaged from politics, being unable to determine who rules over them and what laws are made.

Until very recent times, Britain was able to avoid such a fate because of its combination, unique among European countries, of strong national self-consciousness, sovereign parliamentary democracy and common law. It is precisely these political traditions of Britain's that have rendered its membership of the EU both unnecessary and damaging. Britain needs to reclaim and restore them while it still can. As Arthur Bryant explained so poignantly back in 1963:

> Our history has been so different to that of the Continental nations; as a result of our long island immunity from invasion and the slow, strong growth of our libertarian institutions so much less authoritarian, so much more tolerant, so much gentler than theirs. The Germans *did* find Hitler appealing, *did* tolerate murder and slave-camps for Jews, Slavs, and political opponents, *did* approve of aggressive war so long as it was successful. Even the kindly and gentle Italians were not opposed to their Government's brutal attack on Abyssinia and its cynical declaration of war in 1940. The French, too, like the Germans, accept, as they always have done, police and authoritarian powers in a way that Britons would never tolerate.[55]

For the sake of the prosperity, security and freedom of its inhabitants, present and future, not to mention those who in the past laid down their lives to defend its independence, Britain should withdraw from the European Union.

4

Britain's Best Way
Out of the EU

The last two chapters have surveyed the costs and benefits to Britain of its EU membership. They found that the costs outweigh any benefits by a large margin, both economically and politically. In sum, Britain and its people would be able to enjoy more freedom, justice, democracy, as well as greater prosperity, were it to leave the EU.

In a speech in January 2013, Prime Minister David Cameron pledged that, should his party win the next general election in 2015, a future Conservative government would hold an in/out referendum on British membership after first negotiating new, more favourable terms. The reason the Prime Minister gave for making his pledge was a crisis of legitimacy that he claimed the EU to be facing with the British people. As he put it in his speech: 'Today, public disillusionment with the EU is at an all-time high... The result is that democratic consent for the EU in Britain in now wafer thin... That is why I am in favour of a referendum.'[1]

The reason the Prime Minister gave for wanting to postpone the referendum until after the next election was to gain the time that he claimed was needed to conduct negotiations on the new terms of Britain's membership and without which, he argued, no referendum would be worthwhile. As he put it in his speech: 'I don't believe that to make a decision at this moment is the right way forward... We need to allow some time... so that when the choice comes it will be... between leaving or being part of a new settlement... I believe the best way to do this will be in a new Treaty... But if there is no appetite for a new Treaty... Britain should... address the changes we need in a negotiation with our European partners... And when we have negotiated that new settlement, we will give the British people a referendum with a very simple in or out choice. To stay in the EU on these new terms; or come out altogether.'[2]

Doubtless, in making his referendum pledge, it had been the Prime Minister's primary purpose to place maximum pressure on Britain's other EU partners to yield concessions to Britain, should in the near future a new EU Treaty be sought to resolve the continuing eurocrisis. The price of Britain's agreement to any such new treaty, so the Prime Minister was effectively declaring, would be the several safeguards and economic freedoms to which he made allusion in his speech and of which the chief one would be a guarantee of continued full access for Britain's banks and financial services to the Single Market. At the same time, his referendum pledge was doubtless intended to take the electoral wind out of UKIP's sails by appealing to eurosceptical British voters as offering them their only realistic prospect of being able to secure Britain's withdrawal from the EU. No other mainstream British political party has offered the British electorate a direct vote on the subject since the Labour Party included a similar pledge in its manifesto for the 1974 general election.

Ever since the Prime Minister gave his pledge, the British media have devoted unprecedented attention to all matters relating to Britain's membership of the EU. To date, they have devoted far less attention to considering how Britain might best arrange its departure from the EU should the promised referendum yield a majority vote in favour of its withdrawal, and exactly what future relation the country should seek to forge with the EU upon leaving. The British public, however, can hardly be expected to vote for their country to leave the EU without having first been given some reasonably clear idea as to what they might expect afterwards.

Before David Cameron delivered his referendum pledge, several studies had examined the possible alternative relations Britain might seek to secure with the EU.[3] There was a wide measure of consensus within this body of literature that, should Britain leave the EU, its future relationship with the EU could assume only some variant of one of four different possible forms.

Britain's different possible relationships with the EU upon withdrawal from it

The Norway option
The first possible relationship with the EU that Britain might be able to secure upon leaving is similar to that which Norway, Iceland and Lichtenstein all currently have with it on account of their membership of the European Free Trade Area (EFTA). EFTA was created in 1960 through an initiative of Britain's as an alternative to the EEC. Britain belonged to it until 1973, when it joined the EEC. The special relation with the EU that their EFTA membership confers upon its three members was established through an agreement that they all entered into with the EU in May 1992, when both they and the EU expected all EFTA members would shortly be joining the EU as full members. What the two organisations agreed upon was to create a common economic space that they designated the European Economic Area (EEA).

Intended at the time to encompass all EFTA members, Switzerland, EFTA's fourth current member, has chosen not to be part of the EEA, its citizens having rejected

Swiss membership of the EEA in a referendum held in December 1992. That referendum result also led Switzerland to suspend its application to join the EU. Meanwhile, referendums in Norway in 1994 and 2011 have yielded majority votes against its accession to the EU.

Essentially, the relation with the EU that membership of the EEA confers upon the latter's three EFTA members is full access to the Single Market. In return, as well as having to open their markets reciprocally to EU member states, the three EFTA members of the EEA must also adopt all EU directives and regulations pertaining to the Single Market, and do so without playing any formal part in the drafting or enactment of them.

Dubbed the 'Norway model' on account of Norway's relative prominence among the EEA's three EFTA members, the relation that they have with the EU is also disparagingly referred to by its detractors as 'government by fax'. It is so called on account of their lack of any formal say or participation in the decision-making processes within the EU regarding those of its laws and rules by which, as EEA members, they are bound.

Beyond access to the Single Market, there is one further benefit that their EEA membership gives its three EFTA members which, some might say, more than makes up for their lack of a seat at the EU table at which laws are made about the Single Market. This additional great benefit is that their access to the Single Market comes without any of them having also to be subject to the EU's Common Agricultural Policy, Common Fisheries Policy, the European Court, the European Commission or its Parliament, the shared jurisdiction in the fields of justice and home affairs, or the EU's Common Foreign and Security Policy. Furthermore, the EEA's three EFTA members obtain their access to the Single Market without having to hand over to the EU powers to enter into free trade agreements with non-EU countries.

Those who favour a similar relation for Britain with the EU deny that, in practice, it would lose any real influence over which EU laws it would still be bound by. First, they point out, its current degree of influence is already very limited over laws enacted by the EU, as most are now decided by Qualified Majority Vote. Second, upon leaving the EU, they further point out, Britain would regain, as Norway has never lost, an independent seat on many of the international bodies from which initially emanate, in proposal form, many of the rules and standards eventually adopted by the EU. Hence, should Britain assume a similar relation with the EU as Norway has, it could well end up by gaining in terms of influence over which EU laws it would then be bound by.

That Britain would not lose any real influence in the EU by replacing current membership with a relation more similar to Norway's has been the contention of one of the most vociferous champions of this option. This is Richard North who has contended, as regards Norway's lack of a seat at the EU table, that: 'It is misleading… to assert that… [this] lack equates with Norway being at a disadvantage when compared with the influence exerted by full EU members… In a global trading environment, regulation is being globalised and standard-setting is now shared by many different bodies. Many of these act at a global level. There, Norway has considerable influence, far greater than is exerted by individual EU member states.'[4]

Despite the considerable element of truth in this, Britain might yet be able to retain near full access to the Single Market without its need of having to accept anything like as much EU law and regulation as Norway must, were it able to forge with the EU a relation more similar to that of Switzerland.

The Swiss option
Despite rejecting EEA membership and then suspending its application to join the EU, Switzerland has over the years forged a relation with the EU that several prominent British eurosceptics have claimed would suit Britain much better than any other, especially its current membership. Commencing with a free trade agreement in goods in 1972, Switzerland has managed to negotiate a whole swathe of bilateral agreements with the EU which give it almost full access to the Single Market without having to accept, as the EEA's three EFTA members must do, all EU laws pertaining to the Single Market.

The Conservative MEP Dan Hannan is one of the most fervent advocates of the Swiss option, claiming that: 'Switzerland has most of the benefits of full membership, but... is spared the regulatory burden of Brussels directives... Yes, Swiss exporters must meet EU standards when selling to the EU, just as they must meet Japanese standards when selling to Japan. But they are not obliged to apply these standards, whether to their domestic economy, or to their non-EU exports.'[5]

However attractive the Swiss option might appear, the chances are very slim indeed that Britain might be able to secure a similar relationship with the EU. This is because of the known widespread opposition within the EU to the relation Switzerland has with it on account of its somewhat ad hoc and loose nature. After reviewing it in December 2010, the European Council concluded that: 'while the present system of bilateral agreements has worked well in the past... that system... has become complex and unwieldy to manage and has clearly reached its limits'. [6]

In his 2012 book *Au Revoir Europe: What if Britain left the EU?*, David Charter quotes one unnamed senior Eurocrat as having said of Switzerland's relation with the EU: 'We are not happy with the way we are proceeding... You can imagine, we are not going to repeat this with any other country... It is not totally spelled out, but there is a sentence that says this way of proceeding has reached its limits.'[7]

The Turkish option

A third possible relationship with the EU is similar to that which Turkey has. As a longstanding applicant for full membership, Turkey has in the interim been able to enter into a customs union with the EU. This enables goods to move between Turkey and the EU free of tariff. Turkey is spared having to adopt all of the EU's labour and social legislation

Under a similar arrangement, Britain would be able to make unilateral free trade agreements in connection with services, and would also be able to restrict the entry of nationals of EU states.

Against these distinct advantages have to be set several major disadvantages, not least of which would be that Britain would be obliged to maintain the common EU tariff on all manufactured goods it imports from outside the EU. Additionally, its banks and financial services would no longer have free access to the Single Market. Nor would Britain be able to strike unilateral free-trade agreements with non-EU countries. Additionally, Britain would have 'to swallow whole the EU's rules on product regulation, state aid and competition... all of which are refereed by the European Commission'.[8]

The WTO Option

A further possible relationship that Britain could assume with the EU would be that which it would automatically assume were it to withdraw without first having negotiated any special trade agreement. Its relationship would then be similar to that of all other countries with which it has no such agreement. Such a form of relation is that which the World Trade Organisation designates as 'most favoured nation' status. This status is one that all countries have with one another when there are no special free trade agreements. They have it on account of WTO rules that demand that no country accords another terms of trade any less favourable than those it accords any other country with which it has no free trade agreement or customs union.

Should Britain leave the EU without having first negotiated any free trade agreement with it, then, by these WTO rules, the EU would have to accord Britain such a status. Britain would no longer need to abide by any of the EU's social laws or regulations. Similarly, it could then also restrict migration from the EU, as well as forge unilateral free trade agreements with non-EU countries. However, its exports to the EU would then be subject to the common EU tariff and its citizens would no longer be able to freely work, travel or reside anywhere within the EU as they presently can.

Should Britain assume such a relationship with the EU, then, as Stephen Booth and Christopher Howarth have observed in their 2012 report for Open Europe, *Trading Places: Is EU membership still the best place for UK trade?*:

> [T]here would be a major price to pay... exporters in the UK would suddenly be faced with new tariffs... For example, UK car exports to the EU would be faced with 10 per cent tariffs... and chemical products to the EU would also face problematic tariffs and the restrictive REACH Directives. There would undoubtedly also be pressure from domestic producers... for the UK to impose tariffs on imports... [These] would increase costs for consumers and likely reduce UK trade in the short term.[9]

None of the four options just identified come without very substantial drawbacks. In the case of the Swiss option, not the least of these is that it is almost certainly unavailable to Britain.

However, these four options by no means exhaust the possibilities. Since David Cameron's January 2013 speech, a still more promising fifth option has emerged as a theoretical possibility for Britain, courtesy of Conservative MEP David Campbell Bannerman who has dubbed his preferred option *EEA-Lite*.

The EEA-lite option

Hailed by LSE Professor of European Law Damian Chalmers as 'the first contribution to think seriously and in detail about the legal framework that one would want for a United Kingdom outside the Union',[10] what Campbell Bannerman proposes for Britain is 'a new model for a relationship with the EU based on trade, economics and friendly relations but without political integration'.[11] The full official title he gave the relationship that he proposed is 'Agreement on the European Economic Area (UK Variation)'. Although he considers that it would be desirable for Britain to rejoin the EFTA were it to assume such a relationship with the EU, in his view it would not be strictly necessary to do so:

> EEA Lite is a more flexible version of the existing EEA Agreement between three EFTA states and the EU... 'EEA Lite' differs from EEA Regular in three critical respects:

> 1. The UK will remain a member of the European Economic Area but will leave the single market ('Internal Market') itself – i.e. the UK... will... remain fully open to goods and services from the EU... whilst UK goods and services exported to the EU will still be subject to EU single market rules for the eight per cent of the British economy that trades with the EU, but the UK will be

able to remove these rules for the 92 per cent of the UK economy that does not relate to EU trade, and 80 per cent of which is trade within the UK.

2. The UK will be able to repeal existing EU legislation (*Acquis Communautaire*) and no longer be required to enact new EU legislation... for the 92 per cent of the UK economy that is not concerned with trade with the EU... The UK would also end its membership contributions to the EU of £20 billion a year (£12.2 billion net), though it will make contributions separately through a new UK Grants body to assist Eastern European states to develop.

3. EEA Lite would amend the four key freedoms [of the Single Market] to replace Freedom of Persons by a Freedom of Workers... [This means] those who contribute to national insurance and healthcare provision or who are studying in the UK [could enter, reside and work there] ... but removes any [foreigner's] automatic right to entry to the UK or to receive UK benefits merely because they are EU citizens... This agreement will bring the UK closer to the Swiss position on immigration... enabled by safeguard clauses in the 1999 EU-Swiss bilateral agreement... [which] allow restrictions on long-term residence permits for different EU nations... The caps do not apply to short-term residence visas of up to a year.[12]

Should Britain replace its current EU membership with EEA Lite, and then make an annual per capita contribution to the EU similar to Norway's, but discounted to reflect Britain's considerably lower per capita GDP, Campbell Bannerman estimates that 'the UK would only pay... some £1.5 billion a year. That is just a weighted eight per cent of current UK gross contributions to the EU.'[13]

In favour of EEA Lite, Campbell Bannerman argues

that it has two principal advantages over all other possible post-membership relations with the EU:

> 1. The EEA Agreement is a successful, understandable and workable EU agreement with non-EU European nations, which... makes it an excellent template for negotiations between the UK and the EU towards a more flexible agreement which is more acceptable to the UK

> 2. Under Article 50 of the Lisbon Treaty, an EU member state may withdraw from the EU... [which] is... legally required to negotiate a 'withdrawal agreement/treaty'... with...the departing member... Negotiating this around an existing and proven framework model that already manages the relationship between the EU and non-EU European nations will save negotiating time and speed harmonious negotiations between the EU and UK within this agreed framework. It will also be more palatable to the British public as a more tangible and proven framework for a new relationship outside the EU.[14]

To show how easy it would be to construct, comprehend and work his new proposed settlement for Britain, Campbell Bannerman takes the existing EEA Agreement and, by making only a few critical changes to it, has produced a UK Lite variation. He has published a draft of the amended agreement as a separate appendix to his book on a specially dedicated website: www.timetojump. org

Britain's best strategy for securing a better new relationship with the EU

Of course, Britain is in no position to demand that the EU accords it such a special relationship as EEA Lite or, indeed, any other special relationship, should it decide to leave. Nor, having once begun the withdrawal process by invoking Article 50 of the Lisbon Treaty, could Britain backtrack and unilaterally decide to suspend its withdrawal, should it subsequently discover the EU was unwilling to agree to some special relationship. Furthermore, once it had withdrawn, should Britain subsequently decide that it wanted to re-join the EU, it would have no guarantee, and indeed it would be most unlikely, that it could re-join with the present opt-outs that it currently enjoys from both the Euro and the 135 pre-Lisbon law and home affairs measures. So, the stakes for Britain could not be higher.

There are some, like UKIP MEP Gerard Batten, who argue that it would be folly for Britain to set about withdrawing from the EU by invoking Article 50 of the Lisbon Treaty. This is because it would then become mired in endless negotiations, during which time the British electorate would be subject to a tireless media campaign designed to undermine its confidence in the ability of Britain to survive and prosper outside the EU. Batten writes: 'For two solid years we would have the BBC, elements of the press, the metropolitan political class, and possibly the President of the United States... telling us that EU exit will result in loss of trade, loss of jobs, and calamities of all sorts. How would a Prime Minister hold his nerve under this kind of fire? ... Article 50 is a mechanism to prevent a member state leaving the EU, not one to enable it to do so.'[15] Instead, Batten argues, Britain should simply withdraw unilaterally by repealing the 1972 European Communities Act and then negotiate a new relationship with the EU as a fully independent sovereign country.

It is difficult to see the merits of this proposal. Not only would it profoundly sour Britain's diplomatic relations with the EU for decades, it would also needlessly throw away a powerful bargaining chip that Britain currently has through its EU membership: namely, the ability to veto any future EU Treaty unless it receives a suitably acceptable quid pro quo.

Batten writes of the consequences of his proposed tactic that: 'There will be no loss of jobs or trade … because the EU sells us far more than we sell them, and to put up any discriminatory barriers would be against binding WTO rules. Britain would be in a strong position to agree a trade deal with the EU, but this must be a consequence of leaving; not a condition.' There seems to be a certain amount of unrealistic optimism informing Batten's confidence that the EU would be inclined to accord Britain a free trade agreement, should it leave in this abrupt manner. Indeed, one could even imagine Brussels resorting to some form of sanctions against Britain should it choose to leave in this way that would make life needlessly hard for its nationals, especially those resident abroad within the EU. Far more diplomatic and orderly would be British withdrawal via Article 50 which entails departure two years after its being invoked unless both parties agree to continue negotiations. If the British electorate has seen fit to vote for withdrawal in a referendum on the issue, it is unlikely that it will be persuaded to change its mind once the withdrawal process has begun.

Others maintain that, should Britain decide to withdraw, whether through invoking Article 50 or else simply by repealing the 1972 European Communities Act, it could then quickly and easily secure a new more favourable deal with the EU. Their confidence is grounded on two principal considerations. First, they claim that certain provisions within the Lisbon Treaty oblige the EU to establish free trade agreements and good relations with its neighbours. Second, they claim Britain enjoys great potential bargaining power with the EU on account of the sizable trade deficit it runs with the rest of the EU. Should the EU be unwilling to accord Britain a free trade agreement, their argument runs, the EU would stand to lose more in terms of exports and associated jobs than would Britain. Hence, the EU would have a very strong incentive to offer Britain a free trade agreement. Neither consideration, either singly or jointly, provides a compelling reason to suppose that, should Britain decide to leave the EU, the latter would be either likely in the least to consider itself legally bound or at all disposed to accord Britain a free trade agreement – *outside of the context of negotiations within the EU for a new EU Treaty.*

The relevant provisions in the Lisbon Treaty that some claim oblige the EU to accord Britain a free trade agreement should it leave are Articles 3(5) and Articles (8). Their relevant clauses run:

> In its relations with the wider world, the Union... shall contribute to... free and fair trade... (Article 3 [5])

> The Union shall develop a special relationship with neighbouring countries, aiming to establish an area of prosperity and good neighbourliness... characterised by close and peaceful relations based on cooperation. (Article 8 [1]) [16]

Ian Milne, director of the think-tank Global Britain, is confident that these two Articles of the Lisbon Treaty oblige the EU to accord Britain a free trade agreement should it leave. He bases his confidence in part upon a particular construction he places upon them: 'Note in these two extracts, the word "shall" *obliges* the Union to "contribute to *free and fair trade*" and to "*develop a special relationship etc*"; "may" would not.'[17]

Ingenious as this piece of legerdemain undoubtedly is, it would be rash for Britain to assume that the EU would be at all inclined to place a similar construction upon these two Articles of the Lisbon Treaty. Since the custodian and final arbiter of EU law is the European Court of Justice, which regards its mission to be the advance of European integration, there is little chance that it would feel constrained to interpret the Articles as constitutionally obliging the EU to accord Britain a free trade agreement. Even if the Court were to concede in principle that the Articles did imply such an obligation, in practice negotiations on such a free trade agreement could be protracted indefinitely.

In spite of the claim that Britain's trade deficit with the rest of the EU would make it easy for it to obtain a free trade agreement, the EU is highly unlikely to be minded to accord Britain one, notwithstanding the economic losses that would then be incurred by its member states, especially Germany – the EU's main exporter to Britain. Neither the EU as a whole nor Germany in particular would be in a hurry to accord Britain a free trade agreement if one could possibly be avoided. Both would prefer to let Britain hang in the wind without one to serve as a deterrent to other member states otherwise tempted to follow its example.

There is something that is consistently overlooked by those who invoke the rest of the EU's favourable trade balance with Britain as a reason why the EU would be quick to offer Britain a free trade agreement. What they overlook is how much more there would be at stake for both the EU and Germany than merely their trade surplus with Britain. Both the EU and Germany would want to ensure Britain's departure did not create a precedent or set an example, by ensuring that it did not depart on any terms other than the least favourable possible.

To date, Germany has shown itself both willing and able to shoulder much of the cost associated with servicing the debts of less provident Mediterranean EU members so as to ensure that they remain within the eurozone. There is no reason to suppose that it would not be similarly willing and able to shoulder the further costs that would attend Britain's departure without a free trade agreement in order to ensure that no other member states were tempted to follow suit.

In sum, those who suppose that, because it runs a trade deficit with the rest of the EU, Britain could easily obtain a free trade agreement are guilty of wishful thinking. As Hugo Dixon, Editor-at-Large of Reuter's, has noted:

> Lots of British eurosceptics believe... that it would be easy to retain access to the single market without following its rules. The rest of the EU, they reason, enjoys a big current account surplus with Britain... As a result, the EU will be desperate to do business with Britain and will agree to a relationship much more attractive than what Norway has to put up with. If Britain's post-referendum prime minister bought this line, he or she could be in for a shock. Of course, the EU wouldn't want a trade war. But it would be in a far better position to withstand one than Britain because its economy is six times as big. The EU's exports to the UK may be large, but they amount to only 2.5 percent of its GDP. Britain's exports to the EU amount to 14 per cent of its GDP. If London tried to play hardball, it would probably be sent packing.[18]

Bow Group chairman Ben Harris-Quinney shares Hugo Dixon's doubts about Britain's bargaining power with the EU (outside of the special context of negotiations for a new Treaty). On his organisation's website, Harris-Quinney writes that:

> Even among the most ardent of eurosceptics there continues to be... optimism that core Europe would not seek to punish Britain for going it alone, for fear of damaging their own export economies. This is a potentially catastrophic misunderstanding of how core

Europe, particularly Germany, sees and values the European project. Germany has shown itself willing to underwrite the economy of every eurozone nation, at immense cost, to ensure the future of the project. It is a nation which plans its economy and foreign policy 50 years into the future, and is as a result now defining itself internationally as the world's first soft-power super power through the EU.

For core Europe, if a nation left the EU, and prospered greatly from leaving, the example might be enough to destroy the European project. If that nation failed it might be enough to ensure and galvanize a federal Europe, with no nation risking the harsh climes of life outside of the EU again. If Britain leaves the EU and ventures out alone, seeking to define itself against its former membership, core Europe will undoubtedly seek to make an example, however costly it is in the short term to their export economy.[19]

Of course, if, as seems likely, the euro-crisis continues to blight much of southern Europe to the point at which a new EU Treaty is needed to preserve the euro and the eurozone, then the situation radically alters. Britain's bargaining power with the rest of the EU would then dramatically improve. There is an increasingly promising prospect that Britain will be able to secure a better deal with the EU on the back of a new EU Treaty primarily intended to resolve the euro-crisis. All the elements needed for Britain to be able to secure a new more favourable settlement with the EU are currently lining up in a most auspicious political configuration which may not come by again for a very long time.

Back in October 2013, press reports had begun to circulate that, in the first flush of her re-election victory, German Chancellor Angela Merkel was seeking agreement from her new potential coalition partners in the Social Democratic Party as to the need for a new EU Treaty, as well as for significant concessions to Britain to secure its agreement. The Brussels correspondent of the *Daily Telegraph* Bruno Waterfield reported that:

> The German Chancellor is pushing for a new European Union blueprint to tidy up a "cobweb" of eurozone fiscal rules... agreed... piecemeal... since the debt crisis first threatened Europe's single currency... The German call for treaty change will give the Prime Minister "an opportunity" to demand reform of the EU powers in return for British support... allowing Mr Cameron to present a new settlement with Europe for a 2017 referendum in Britain. Chancellor Merkel... will kick off negotiations towards treaty change at a Brussels summit in late June 2014.[20]

Alongside press reports of Chancellor Merkel's plan for EU Treaty reform, it was also being reported that the eurosceptic Conservative MP Douglas Carswell had warned David Cameron that, should any new Treaty be in the offing: 'many Conservatives would be expecting an exemption for British companies trading outside the EU from all Brussels regulation and allowing Britain to sign its own international trade deals'.[21] These are precisely the terms of Campbell Bannerman's proposed EEA Lite agreement.

Some expressed doubts that the German Chancellor would be able to secure the agreement of her prospective coalition partners to concessions to Britain. *Der Spiegel* reported that the deputy leader of the parliamentary group of the German Social Democratic Party had said: 'The SPD won't support any arrangements if Merkel conducts parallel negotiations with Britain's David Cameron to transfer EU powers back to member states.'[22]

At the time, the reluctance of Germany's Social Democrats to agree concessions to Britain led some to doubt whether Chancellor Merkel would pursue her desired reforms of the eurozone through Treaty change, thereby depriving Britain of the opportunity to obtain major concessions. Mats Persson, director of the think-tank Open Europe, for example, was quoted as having said: 'Leverage shouldn't be overstated as... [there is] a risk that Merkel will seek arrangements outside the ordinary EU treaties, in effect circumventing the UK.'[23]

In December 2013, however, the German Chancellor reiterated her belief in the need for a new treaty. In her opening address to the German parliament, she said: 'I know that pushing through treaty changes in the member states can be difficult, but if you want more Europe, you have to be prepared to develop it further. In a world that is constantly changing, we can't stand there and say that at some point we agreed the Lisbon Treaty and there's no need to change it again. This won't work.'[24] By late February 2014, it was being reported that 'Downing Street believes that Angela Merkel will... back David Cameron's attempt to renegotiate Britain's relationship with the European Union.'[25]

It therefore seems that Britain is about to acquire a rare window of opportunity through which it might be able to secure the likes of EEA Lite, provided that it plays its negotiating cards well. As Douglas Carswell remarked with reference to the current referendum lock on any new EU Treaty: 'The referendum means that the EU will be negotiating with the British people.'[26]

If a British referendum is guaranteed, then Britain has the ability to obtain a new better settlement with the EU, given how sceptical of the EU the British people are known to be. It is, thus, within the context of EU negotiations for a new Treaty that Britain's best prospects lie for being able to regain the economic and political freedoms it has lost to Brussels without having to forgo continued full access to the Single Market.

In sum, the future relationship that Britain should be seeking to secure with the EU is that set out in David Campbell Bannerman's proposed EEA Lite arrangement, and Britain's best prospect for securing it lies in the context of negotiations for a new EU Treaty needed to resolve the euro-crisis. Outside of such a context, the prospect remains very small that Britain might be able to obtain some such new settlement as EEA Lite. So, too, it must be faced, are the chances that the British electorate would be willing to vote in favour of Britain's withdrawal from the EU in a referendum without its having first obtained a cast-iron guarantee from the EU of continued access to the Single Market upon its withdrawal.

Deploying the 'Adenauer gambit' as Britain's best negotiating tactic

It is by no means without precedent in the history of European integration for major treaties to be linked to other more local treaties in the manner that is being proposed here. An example is provided by a pair of treaties, now largely forgotten, that were signed in Paris on two successive days in May 1952. The parties to these treaties were the three western allied powers, Britain, America and France, on the one hand, and on the other, West Germany. The first treaty was the so-called 'General Treaty' whose full official title was the 'Convention on Relations with the Federal Republic of Germany'. The second treaty was the ill-fated European Defence Community (EDC) Treaty, signed by the foreign secretaries of all four countries that were party to it, but which the French National Assembly then declined to ratify in August 1954.

The General Treaty accorded the West German Chancellor something he had been seeking for some time.

This was an end to the allied occupation regime and full sovereignty in international affairs for the fledgling West German Republic. The other treaty, which Adenauer refused to agree without agreement to the General Treaty, was an agreement by its four parties to the creation of a West European army that was to include a contingent of German troops.

The idea of creating a West European army containing German troops had first been proposed among the western allies at the commencement of the Korean War in June 1950. The French, however, had rejected an offer by Chancellor Adenauer in September 1950 to raise twelve divisions as Germany's contribution to such an army. A month later, however, France appeared to relent somewhat, after its Prime Minister Rene Pleven proposed to the French National Assembly the creation of a European army under a High Authority similar to that which the Schuman Declaration had proposed for the European Coal and Steel Community. Adenauer was cleverly able to exploit the desire of the three western allies, especially America, for a European army, so as to secure their agreement to the terms of the General Treaty that he so badly wanted. As Adenauer's biographer Charles Williams explains:

> There is no doubt that Adenauer... thought that some sort of West German military capability was a precondition of full political sovereignty... But, whatever the basis for his claim that there was a 'Russian threat to the Western World', by the end of 1949 Adenauer's rhetoric was being heard with dismay by the French and British... The rearmament issue remained quiescent until the outbreak of the Korean War on June 25th 1950.... [when] Adenauer's arguments in favour of West German rearmament... took on new force...[The war] forced the Americans to reconsider their previous position on West

German rearmament... Adenauer was quick to grasp an opportunity for the new West Germany. To put it bluntly, there was a case for blackmail, however gently expressed...

During the summer of 1951... [Germany was] in almost constant negotiation with... the Allied governments to see what, if anything, could be salvaged from the Pleven Plan [for a European Army with a contingent of West German forces]. By the end of July an interim report had been agreed between all parties. A 'European Defence Community' was to be set up, which would incorporate a German contingent... But it was not enough [for Adenauer] ... There should [also] be... he said a general treaty which would recognise West German sovereignty, accept German contingents into the EDC on an equal footing, allow West German entry into NATO, end the Occupation Statute and conclude a peace treaty [with Germany]...

But when... [the text of a treaty reflecting Adenauer's views] was handed to the High Commissioners [of the three western allies] on 30 August, the reception was icy... But Adenauer was playing from strength... He [declared]... that there would be no German agreement on the EDC unless there were agreement on a treaty incorporating the provisions which Adenauer had given out... The two treaties were, he said, interlinked. The gambit was effective. The Allies agreed to parallel discussions on both treaties... [These discussions] went surprisingly quickly; by the end of November 1951 the General Treaty was ready in draft and detailed agreements had been reached to set up the EDC... By then it was evident that Adenauer had achieved almost all he wanted... [Although] the [General] Treaty was not signed until May 1952... the principle of the simultaneous signature of the General Treaty and the EDC Treaty, and the interlinking of the two, had been firmly established.'[27]

When it comes to securing for itself a new, more favourable relation with the EU, Britain would do well to take a leaf out of Germany's book. In its negotiations with the EU, it should adopt the same gambit as was used by Germany's 'sly old fox' (as Adenauer was known) to extract agreement from the western allies to terms of a treaty that he wanted and was able to obtain by making their agreement the price of his willingness to agree another treaty that they wanted with West Germany.

There would be supreme irony, and not a little historical justice, should Britain regain the powers that it has lost to the EU by adopting the same stratagem as was so successfully employed to recover lost German sovereignty by the very same statesman whose initial call for Franco-German union in March 1950 led, via the Schuman Declaration, to the creation of the very European supranational organisation that for so long has steadily been diminishing Britain's sovereignty. Recourse to the Adenauer gambit would form a supremely fitting way for Britain to end its membership of the EU upon the best terms possible. Recounting that gambit is therefore an appropriate way to bring the present study to an end.

Notes

Introduction

1 Torreblanca, J.I. and Leonard, M., 'The remarkable rise of continental Euroscepticism', *Guardian*, 24 April 2013: http://www.guardian.co.uk/commentisfree/2013/apr/24/continental-euroscepticism-rise

2 'David Cameron's EU Speech in full', *Telegraph*, 23 January 2013: http://www.telegraph.co.uk/news/worldnews/europe/eu/9820230/David-Camerons-EU-speech-in-full.html

3 Parkinson, J., Wilkins, L. and Caulkett, M., 'Vote 2013', BBC News: http://www.bbc.co.uk/news/uk-politics-21240020

4 Martin, R. and Higginson, J., 'Michael Gove and Philip Hammond break ranks to expose Tory Europe splits', *Metro*, 12 May 2013: http://metro.co.uk/2013/05/12/dont-back-the-euro-rebels-david-cameron-tells-ministers-before-free-vote-3755767/

5 Martin, R. and Higginson, J., 'Michael Gove and Philip Hammond break ranks to expose Tory Europe splits', *Metro*, 12 May 2013: http://metro.co.uk/2013/05/12/dont-back-the-euro-rebels-david-cameron-tells-ministers-before-free-vote-3755767/

6 'End the drift in our relationship with Europe', *Telegraph*, 9 December 2012: http://www.telegraph.co.uk/comment/telegraph-view/9730447/End-the-drift-in-our-relationship-with-Europe.html

7 Brogan, B. and Winnett, R., 'Owen Paterson: We want our country back from Europe', *Telegraph*, 8 December 2012: http://www.telegraph.co.uk/news/politics/9731057/Owen-Paterson-We-want-our-country-back-from-Europe.html

8 Ross, T., 'Boris Johnson: leaving Europe a shot in the arm for democracy', *Telegraph*, 9 May 2013: http://www.telegraph.co.uk/news/politics/10046990/Boris-Johnson-leaving-Europe-a-shot-in-the-arm-for-democracy.html

9 Mulholland, H. and Sparrow, A., 'Ken Clarke warns of "folly" of putting Britain's EU membership at risk', *Guardian*, 19 November 2012: http://www.guardian.co.uk/world/2012/nov/19/ken-clarke-folly-britain-eu

10 Office of the Press Secretary, 'Readout of the President's Call with Prime Minister Cameron of the United Kingdom', The White House, 17 January 2013: http://www.whitehouse.gov/the-press-office/2013/01/17/readout-president-s-call-prime-minister-cameron-united-kingdom

11 Czuczka, T., 'Merkel Says U.K. Is Important Partner That Should Stay in EU', *Bloomberg*, 16 May 2013: http://www.bloomberg.com/news/2013-05-16/merkel-parties-block-carbon-fix-talks-on-election-year-split-1-.html

12 Henry, S., 'Europe can survive without Britain, says François Hollande', *Telegraph*, 16 May 2013: http://www.telegraph.co.uk/news/worldnews/francois-hollande/10062935/Europe-can-survive-without-Britain-says-Francois-Hollande.html

13 Lawson, N., 'I'll be voting to quit the EU', *Times*, 7 May 2013.

14 Portillo, M., 'We don't share Europe's vision. So I want out', *Times*, 9 May 2013.

15 Heseltine, M., 'Britain must take the lead in Europe, not decline outside', *Financial Times*, 10 May 2013.

16 Borger, J., 'EU exit would put US trade deal at risk, Britain warned', *Guardian*, 27 May 2013.

17 'Remarks by President Obama and Prime Minister Cameron of the United Kingdom in Joint Press Conference', Press Release, The White House, Office, 13 May 2013.

18 See Dreyfuss, R., *Devil's Game: How the United States Helped Unleash Fundamentalist Islam* (New York: Metropolitan Books, 2005).

19 Kyle, K., *Suez*, Second Revised Edition, London and New York: I.B.Tauris, 2003, p.467.

20 Gerard Schröder, 'Germany Can Only Lead Europe the Way Porcupines Mate', *Spiegel on Line*, 1 April 2013: http://www.spiegel.de/international/germany/interview-former-german-chancellor-gerhard-schroeder-on-foreign-policy-a-891839.html

21 'Final Report of the Future of Europe Group', 17 September 2012: http://www.auswaertiges-amt.de/cae/servlet/contentblob/626338/publicationFile/171844/120918-Abschlussbericht-Zukunftsgruppe.pdf

22 'Van Rompuy to Cameron: "We have an exit clause"', *EurActiv.com*, 1 March 2013: http://www.euractiv.com/uk-europe/van-rompuy-cameron-exit-clause-news-518163

23   Juncker, J-C, 'My Priorities', EPP Website, 23 April 2014:
     http://juncker.epp.eu/my-priorities
24   Lord Hannay in interview with Jonathan J. Lindsell, 10 June
     2013, in Lindsell, J., 'The Prospects of an EU Renegotiation and
     Referendum', *Civitas*, 5 July 2013:
     http://civitas.org.uk/pdf/TheProspectsofEURenegotiation.pdf

1: The European Union: its Origins and Rationale

1   Three examples of the received history of the EU: (1) 'How to
     prevent a recurrence of... wars [between Germany and France]
     ... occupied many minds... in the immediate post-war period...
     [One] possible solution... was that Germany... should be linked
     so organically with its neighbours... that another war between
     the nations of Western Europe would become impossible...
     [T]he most clear-sighted and persuasive advocate of this
     approach was a Frenchman, Jean Monnet... indisputably ...
     principal architect [of European unity]... In 1950 his moment
     of destiny came: it was his proposal [that the West German and
     the French coal and steel industries should be placed under a
     single High Authority] that... has been the essential condition
     for all subsequent progress towards European unity.' [Leonard,
     D., *Pocket Guide to the European Community* (Oxford and New York:
     Basil Blackwell, 1988; revised edition 1989), pp.4–5.] (2)
     '[T]he ECSC... was Monnet's ingenious solution to the problem
     of coexisting and conducting business securely with Germany...
     [It] created a Franco-German alliance that has endured for 60
     years and laid the basis for peace and prosperity in Western
     Europe since 1950.' [Dedman, M.J., *The Origins and Development
     of the European Union 1945–2008*, 2nd Edition (London and New
     York, Routledge, 2010), pp.55–56.] (3) 'As early as 1917... Jean
     Monnet... was already beginning to argue passionately that
     there was a need for collective action to solve problems that no
     state could deal with on its own... thinking ... that became the
     basis of the concrete proposals made in the Schuman Declaration
     of 9 May 1950, which was the basis of the first Community, the
     European Coal and Steel Community, which in turn led to the
     European Economic Community and, in 1993, the European
     Union.' Nicoll, W. and Salmon, T. C., *Understanding the European
     Union* (Harlow, Essex: Pearson Education, 2001), pp.8–9.]
2   Two illustrative quotations show how well-entrenched the now
     received account of the EU's origins has become: 'Movements

to unite Europe politically only emerged post-World War I. The horror and carnage of World War I was the motivation behind this wish to end the destructive antagonistic rivalry of European nation states... World War II... changed everything. It increased support for federal ideas... A federal state with supranational powers was invariably advocated by non-communist wartime Resistance movements... There is continuity in aim and rationale between the Resistance, the post-war European federalist movements and some organisations and institutions... created between 1947 and 1957... [that show] that the wartime's Resistance agenda for post-war Europe had an enduring logic and relevance.' [Dedman, M., *The Origins and Development of the European Union 1945–2008: A History of European Integration* (London and New York, 2010), pp.14–16]; 'A major impetus [for European integration] ... was the horror of the First World War... The totalitarian and dictatorial nature of fascism and National Socialism pushed the idea of European union into the background and, indeed into another catastrophic war... [B]efore the war had ended radical thinking was taking place in the resistance movements of Europe, as those involved did not want a return to the past.'. [Nicoll, W. Sir and Salmon, T.C., *Understanding the European Union* (Harlow, Essex: Longman, 2001), 6–9 *passim*.]

3 Salewski, M., 'Ideas of the National Socialist Government and Party' in Lipgens, W., *Documents on the History of European Integration, Vol. 1: Continental Plans for European Union 1939–45* (Berlin: Walter de Grayter and Co., 1984), p.42.

4 Seyss-Inquart, A., 'Speech on Assuming Governmental Authority', 29 May 1940, quoted in Lipgens, W., *Documents on the History of European Integration*, pp.72–73.

5 Seyss-Inquart, A., 'Programme Speech', quoted in Lipgens, W., *Documents on the History of European Integration*, pp.72–73.

6 Hunke, H., 'Introduction' to (eds.) Society of Berlin and Commerce and the Berlin School of Economics, *European Economic Community*, (Berlin: Haude & Spenesche Verlasbuchhandlung Max Paschke, 1942), *passim*: http://homepage.ntlworld.com/lee.riley/Notices/EWG.pdf

7 Thompson, D., 'The World Germanica', *New York Herald Tribune*, 31 March 1940.

8 Hank, R., 'We Europeans: After the loss of innocence', *Eurozine*, 17 January 2014 (first published in German in *Merkur* 10 November 2013):

http://www.eurozine.com/articles/2014-01-17-hank-en.html

9   Dedman, M.J., *The Origins and Development of the European Union*, p.14.

10 Mises, L., *Omnipotent Government: The Rise of the Total State and Total War*, first published 1944 (Spring Mills, PA: Libertarian Press Inc: 1985), p.153.

11 Andler, C., *Pan-Germanism: Its plans for German expansion in the World* (Paris: Librarie Aemand Colin, 1915), p.6:
    http://libcudl.colorado.edu/wwi/pdf/i73472050.pdf

12 Eckardt, J. von, *Berlin-Vienna-Rome: Reflections on the new course and the new situation in Europe* (1892), p.89, quoted in Andler, C., *Pan-Germanism*, p.7.

13 Hesse, E., *Weltpolitik* (Deutsche Politik, part V), pp.65–67, quoted in Andler, C., *Pan-Germanism*, p.28 and p.52.

14 Willhelm II, 'Order of the day ', found in the possession of German prisoners taken in the Bzura in June 1915; quoted in Andler, C., *Pan-Germanism*, p.81.

15 List, F., *The National System of Political Economy*, first published 1844, trans. Lloyd, S.S., (London: Longmans, Green and Co., 1909). Chapter XXXV Continental Politics:
    http://oll.libertyfund.org/title/315/30316/703267

16 List, F., *The National System of Political Economy*, Chapter XXXV Continental Politics.

17 Winkler, P., *The Thousand-Year Conspiracy: Social Germany Behind the Mask* (New York: Charles Scribner's Sons, 1943), pp.4–16 *passim*.

18 Schuman, R., 'Declaration' , 9 May 1950:
    http://www.schuman.info/

19 Quoted in Monnet, J., *Memoirs* (London: Collins, 1978), p.285.

20 Jean Monnet: 'Basically... I shared Adenauer's views... Adenauer... wanted to sublimate national rivalry over the coal and steel resources by uniting Germany and France. This idea of a prior global union, intended to envelop and remove a particular difficulty, was not in my view very realistic. On the contrary, it seemed to me, we should start with the difficulty, using it as a lever to initiate a more general solution. Unity would gradually be created by the momentum of a first achievement. Our efforts must therefore be concentrated in the very point about which disagreements had come to a head.' Monnet, J., *Memoirs*, p.286.

21 Adenauer, K., Speech at Christian Democratic Party Meeting, 1946, quoted in Vogel, B. and Buchstab, G., Preface, eds.

Buchstab, G. and Schreiner, R. (eds.), *Konrad Adenauer and the European Integration* (Berlin: Konrad Adenauer Foundation, 2007):
http://www.kas.de/upload/ACDP/GB_Katalog_KA.pdf

22 Monnet, J., *Memoirs*, p.311.

23 Evans-Pritchard, A., 'Euro-federalists financed by US spy chiefs', *Telegraph*, 19 September 2000:
http://www.telegraph.co.uk/news/worldnews/europe/1356047/
Euro-federalists-financed-by-US-spy-chiefs.html

24 Dorril, S., *MI6: Fifty Years of Special Operations* (London: Fourth Estate, 2000), p.496.

25 Dorril, S., *MI6: Fifty Years of Special Operations*, p.508.

26 Aldrich, R.J., *The Hidden Hand: Britain, America and Cold War Secret Intelligence* (London: John Murray, 2001), pp.342–344 *passim*.

27 Tetens, T.H., *Germany Plots with the Kremlin*, 1953, pp.viii–ix.

28 Tetens, T.H., *Germany Plots with the Kremlin*, p.95.

29 Quoted in Tetens, T.H., *Germany Plots with the Kremlin*, p.103.

30 Marsh, D., *Germany and Europe: The Crisis of Unity*, first published, 1994, (London: Mandarin, 1995), p.151.

31 Nicholas Ridley, quoted in Lawson, D., 'Saying the Unsayable About the Germans', *Spectator*, 14 July 1990, pp.8–9.

32 Lawson, D., 'Ridley was right', *Spectator*, 24 September 2011.

33 Mises, L., *Omnipotent Government*, pp.278–282 *passim*.

34 Public Records Office (PRO), FO 371/150369; quoted in Mullen, A. and Burkitt, B., 'Spinning Europe: Pro-European Union Propaganda Campaigns in Britain, 1962–1975', *Political Quarterly*, 2005, 76 (1), 100–113; pdf version, p.3.

35 Quoted in Wolfram, K., 'To Join or Not to Join: the Appeasement Policy of Britain's First EEC Application' in Brivati, B. and Jones, H., (eds.), *From Reconstruction to Integration: Britain and Europe Since 1945* (London: Leicester University Press, 1993), 144–156, p.145.

36 Taylor, A.J.P., 'Macmillan Has Not Found the Answer Yet', *Sunday Times*, 15 June 1962:
http://www.brugesgroup.com/mediacentre/index.
live?article=115#macmillan

37 PRO, CAB 128/36, CC (62) (62), 48; quoted in Mullen, A. and Burkitt, B., 'Spinning Europe', p.4.

38 Shore, P., *Separate Ways: The Heart of Europe* (London: Duckworth, 2000), pp.5–6.

39 Shore, P., *Separate Ways*, pp.8–9.

40 Shore, P., *Separate Ways*, p.13.

41 Shore, P., *Separate Ways*, pp.13–14.

42 Mullen, A. and Burkitt, B., 'Spinning Europe', p.11.

43 Mullen, A. and Burkitt, B., 'Spinning Europe', pp.11–12.

44 Body, B., *England for the English* (London: New European Publications, 2001), p.118.

45 Meyer, C., *Facing Reality: From World Federation to the Central Intelligence Agency* (New York: HarperCollins, 1980).

2: The Economic Costs and Benefits of Membership

1 Wistrich, E., *The United States of Europe* (London and New York: Routledge, 1994), pp.1–5 *passim*.

2 Wistrich, E., *The United States of Europe*, pp.136–151 *passim*.

3 This point is made, for example, by minister without portfolio Kenneth Clarke in the *Telegraph*, 22 May 2014:
http://www.telegraph.co.uk/news/worldnews/europe/eu/10850642/Quitting-EU-would-hurt-business-says-Kenneth-Clarke.html
The jobs argument was recently advanced by British Influence in a report published on its behalf by the Centre for Economics and Business Research (Cebr)), entitled 'UK jobs supported by experts to the EU' (London: Cebr, March 2014):
http://www.cebr.com/reports/british-jobs-and-the-single-market/

4 CBI, *Our Global Future: The business vision for a reformed EU* (London: CBI, 2013):
http://www.cbi.org.uk/media/2451423/our_global_future.pdf

5 See, for example, Nick Clegg's view in Faulconbridge, G., 'Clegg dismisses Cameron's EU strategy as "wishful thinking"', Reuters, 09 May 2014:
http://uk.reuters.com/article/2014/05/09/uk-britain-politics-clegg-idUKKBN0DO1NN20140509

6 TheCityUK, *A legal assessment of the UK's relationship with the EU: a financial services perspective*, April 2014:
http://www.thecityuk.com/research/our-work/reports-list/a-legal-assessment-of-the-uk-s-relationship-with-the-eu

7 See, for example, the speech by Liberal Democrats' President Tim Farron on 9 April 2014, 'There's only one party that the party of IN' (Liberal Democrats Website, 10 April 2014):
http://www.libdems.org.uk/tim_farron_there_s_only_one_party_that_s_the_party_of_in

See also CBI, *Our Global Future*, p.79.

8   Source: Office for Budget Responsibility and H.M.Treasury as cited in H.M.Treasury, European Union Finances 2013, Cm 8740, November 2013, Table 3.A, p.14.

9   CBI, *Our Global Future*, p.11

10 CBI, *Our Global Future*, p.78–80

11 Burrage, M., *Where's the Insider Advantage? A comparative study of UK exports to EU and non-EU nations between 1960 and 2012*, (Civitas, London, 2014): http://www.civitas.org.uk/pdf/insideradvantage.pdf

12 Bootle, R., *The Trouble With Europe*, (London: Nicholas Brealey, 2014), especially chapter 3

13 Gaskell, S. and Persson, M., *Still Out of Control?* (London: Open Europe 2010), p.10: http://www.openeurope.org.uk/Content/documents/Pdfs/stilloutofcontrol.pdf

Congdon, T., *How much does the European Union cost Britain?* (UKIP, 2012), p.49.

14 Niemietz, K., 'Abolish the CAP, let food prices tumble', Institute of Economic Affairs Website, 13 January 2013: http://www.iea.org.uk/blog/abolish-the-cap-let-food-prices-tumble

15 Rotherham, L., *The Price of Fish – Costing the Common Fisheries Policy* (London: Taxpayers' Alliance, 2009), p.7: http://www.taxpayersalliance.com/CFP.pdf

16 Burrage, M., *Where's the Insider Advantage?*, pp.41 – 62.

17 Burrage, M., *Where's the Insider Advantage?* , pp.41–57.

18 Burrage, M., *The EU Effect: The impact of the EU on foreign direct investment in the UK from 1970 to 2011*, London: Civitas, 2014

19 Stewart, E., *The UK's Unique Trading Opportunity* (London: Global Britain, 2014): http://www.globalbritain.co.uk/sites/default/files/publications/THE%20UK%27s%20%20Unique%20Trading%20Opportunity.pdf

20 Oxford Economics, commissioned by the CBI, *The economic impact for the EU of a Solvency II inspired funding regime for pension funds*, (Oxford: Economics, 2012): http://www.cbi.org.uk/media/1886242/oe_1cbi_pensions_report_2012_final_copy_pdf_pdf.pdf

21 Geddes, A., *Britain and the European Union*, p.170.

22 A very comprehensive statement of the countervailing case against both presuppositions is to be found in Idso, C.C, Carter,

R.M. and Singer, S.F., *Climate Change Reconsidered II: Physical Science, 2013 Report of the Nongovernmental International Panel on Climate Change* (Chicago: The Heartland Institute, 2013): http://heartland.org/media-library/pdfs/CCR-II/CCR-II-Full.pdf See Summary for Policymakers: http://heartland.org/media-library/pdfs/CCR-II/Summary-for-Policymakers.pdf

23 Lawson, N., *An Appeal to Reason: A Cool Look at Global Warming* (London and New York: Duckworth, 2009), p.114.

24 Open Europe, *The EU Climate Action and Renewable Energy Package: Are we about to be locked into the wrong policy?* (London: Open Europe, 2008): http://www.openeurope.org.uk/Content/Documents/PDFs/carep.pdf

25 Craig, D. and Elliott, M., *The Great European Rip-Off* (London: Random House Books, 2009), pp.254–255.

26 Nicola, S. and Andresen, T., 'Merkel's Green Shift Forces Germany to Burn More Coal', Bloomberg, 20 August 2012: http://www.bloomberg.com/news/2012-08-19/merkel-s-green-shift-forces-germany-to-burn-more-coal-energy.html

27 Open Europe submission to the UK Government's Balance of Competences Review: Environment and Climate Change synopsis, August 2013: http://www.openeurope.org.uk/Content/Documents/Open_Europe_submission_Environment_and_Climate_Change.pdf

28 Booth, S., Howarth, C., Persson, M., and Scarpetta, V., *Continental Shift: Safeguarding the UK's financial trade in a changing Europe* (London: Open Europe, 2001), p.3.

29 Vaubel, R., 'EU Financial Market Regulation': A Strategy of Raising Rivals' Costs', Speech to the Bruges Group, 6 November 2010;

30 Quoted in Hough, A., 'Nicholas Sarkozy hails EU appointment to "clamp down on City of London"', *Telegraph*, 2 December 2009: http://www.telegraph.co.uk/news/worldnews/europe/france/6666188/Nicolas-Sarkozy-hails-EU-appointment-to-clamp-down-on-City-of-London.html

31 Waterfield, B., 'France runs into trouble in wrangle for Brussels job', *Telegraph*, 25 November 2009: http://www.telegraph.co.uk/news/worldnews/europe/eu/6654612/France-runs-into-trouble-in-wrangle-for-Brussels-jobs.html

32 Warmoll, C., 'Bank bonus cap will "damage" UK and EU

competitiveness', *Accountancy Live*, 6 March 2013:
http://www.accountancylive.com/croner/jsp/editorialDetails/
category/In-Practice/Development/editorial/Bank-bonus-cap-
will-damage-UK-and-EU-competitiveness

33 Warmoll, C., 'Bank bonus cap will "damage" UK and EU
competitiveness'.

34 Waterfield, B., 'UK anger over "secret" EU financial transaction
tax plan', *Telegraph*, 6 May 2014:
http://www.telegraph.co.uk/finance/newsbysector/
banksandfinance/10810978/UK-anger-over-secret-EU-financial-
transaction-tax-plan.html

35 Waterfield, B., 'UK anger over "secret" EU financial transaction
tax plan'.

36 Laja, S., 'EU Tobin tax could force portfolio rejig', *Financial Times*,
8 August 2013:
http://www.ft.com/cms/s/0/56852ee8-0028-11e3-ba6b-
00144feab7de.html?siteedition=uk

37 'This latest blow to the FT further vindicates the Treasury's
opposition', *Telegraph*, 1 September 2013:
http://www.telegraph.co.uk/finance/newsbysector/
banksandfinance/10300365/Blow-to-the-FTT-vindicates-the-
Treasury.html

38 Armitstead, L., 'EU lawyers say financial transaction tax is
illegal', *Telegraph*, 10 September 2013:
http://www.telegraph.co.uk/finance/newsbysector/
banksandfinance/10300364/EU-lawyers-say-financial-
transaction-tax-is-illegal.html

39 European Central Bank, 'The Eurosystem policy principles
on the location and operation of infrastructures settling euro-
denominated payment transactions':
http://www.ecb.europa.eu/pub/pdf/other/eurosystem_policy_
principlesen.pdf

40 ECB, 'Eurosystem Oversight Policy Framework', July 2011:
http://www.ecb.europa.eu/pub/pdf/other/
eurosystemoversightpolicyframework2011en.pdf

41 Boyfield, K., 'New Threats to London's Euro-Dominance', *Wall
Street Journal*, 30 September 2012:
http://online.wsj.com/article/SB10000872396390443916104578
022090468435254.html

42 Association of British Insurers, *UK Insurance: Key Facts* (London:
Association of British Insurers, 2012), p.3.

43 Hodgson, J., 'The UK Insurance Industry and the EU', in Lawlor,

S. (ed.), *The Financial Sector and the UK Economy: The Danger of Over Regulation* (London: Politeia, 2013), pp.39–40.

44 Oxford Economics, *The economic impact for the EU of a Solvency II-inspired funding regime for pension funds.*

45 Oxford Economics, *The economic impact for the EU of a Solvency II-inspired funding regime for pension funds.*

46 'EU pension changes would slash jobs and growth – CBI', CBI Press Release, 1 December 2012: http://www.cbi.org.uk/media-centre/press-releases/2012/12/eu-pension-changes-would-slash-jobs-and-growth-cbi/

47 Ollrog, M., 'Fund Managers Afraid of AIFM Directive', *CFO Insight*, 8 August 2012: http://www.cfo-insight.com/financing-liquidity/equity/fund-managers-afraid-of-aifm-directive/

48 Cochrane, S., 'The EU, the UK and the Financial Sector-Renegotiating the Future' in Lawlor, S. (ed.), *The Financial Sector and the UK Economy*, 41–46, pp.42–43.

49 Congdon, T., *How Much Does the European Union Cost Britain?* (UKIP, 2013), pp.36–38. The order of the last two paragraphs of this quotation has been transposed: http://www.timcongdon4ukip.com/docs/UKIP%20Cost%20of%20the%20EU.pdf

50 Congdon, T., *How Much does the European Union cost Britain?*, p.39.

51 Congdon, T., *How Much does the European Union cost Britain?*, p.39.

52 Congdon, T., *How Much does the European Union cost Britain?*, p.41, fn.2.

53 Scholefield, A., *Warning: Immigration Can Seriously Damage Your Wealth* (London: Social Affairs Unit, 2007), p.16.

54 'Romanian and Bulgarian Migration: Dip in Workers Coming to UK', 14 May 2014, BBC Website: http://www.bbc.co.uk/news/uk-27407126

55 Migration Watch UK, 'Press Comment on the latest Immigration Statistics', 22 May 2014: http://www.migrationwatchuk.org/press-release/387

56 Nigel Farage in Interview with Sara Firth, '"Are my children going to grow up in a country that they can call their own?" – UKIP leader', *RT Newsweek*, 4 March 2013: http://rt.com/op-edge/uk-eu-membership-ukip-farage-801/

57 Ross, T., 'Migrants cost up to £8k each in NHS care, schools and welfare', *Telegraph*, 8 December 2013: http://www.telegraph.co.uk/news/politics/10503178/Migrants-cost-up-to-8k-each-in-NHS-care-schools-and-welfare.html

This figure relates to all migrants to the UK, not specifically European Union migrants.

58 Osborn, A., 'UK clashes with EU over plan to curb migrant benefits', Reuters, 27 November 2013: http://uk.reuters.com/article/2013/11/27/uk-britain-immigration-eu-idUKBRE9AQ0AW20131127

59 Slack, J., 'Migrant cap? Cut Britain's generous benefits instead! Top Eurocrat's stinging reply to Theresa May's proposal', *Mail*, 5 December 2013: http://uk.reuters.com/article/2013/11/27/uk-britain-immigration-eu-idUKBRE9AQ0AW20131127

3: The Political Costs and Benefits of Membership

1 Margaret Thatcher in TV Interview for Granada, *World in Action*, 27 January 1978: http://www.margaretthatcher.org/document/103485

2 Churchill, W., Speech, Zurich, 19 September 1946: http://assembly.coe.int/Main.asp?link=/AboutUs/zurich_e.htm

3 Adenauer, K., 'End of Nationalism' in Adenauer, K., *World Indivisible, with Liberty and Justice for All*, trans. Winston, R. & C. (New York: Harper and Brothers, 1955), p.6: http://ia600305.us.archive.org/13/items/worldindivisible007073mbp/worldindivisible007073mbp.pdf

4 Speech by Chancellor Helmut Kohl on the Occasion of the Conferral of His Honorary Doctorate by the Catholic University of Leuven, Belgium, 2 February 1996; in *Bulletin* (Press and Information Office of the Federal Government), no. 12, February 8, 1966, reprinted in *Internationale Politik*, no. 8, 1966, pp.82–84; trans. Brown, A.

5 Waterfield, B., 'Herman Van Rompuy: "Euroscepticism leads to war"', *Telegraph*, 10 November 2010: http://www.telegraph.co.uk/news/worldnews/europe/eu/8124189/Herman-Van-Rompuy-Euroscepticism-leads-to-war.html

6 'Jean-Claude Juncker Interview: "The Demons Haven't Been Banished"', *Der Spiegel*, 1 March 2013: http://www.spiegel.de/international/europe/spiegel-interview-with-luxembourg-prime-minister-juncker-a-888021.html

7 Barroso, J.M.D., 'State of the Union address 2013', European Parliament plenary session, Strasbourg, 1 September 2013:

http://europa.eu/rapid/press-release_SPEECH-13-684_en.htm

8   Hopkins, N., 'UK would jeopardise military standing by leaving
    EU, says German minister', *Guardian*, 22 April 2013:
    http://www.theguardian.com/world/2013/apr/22/uk-military-
    eu-german-minister

9   Morgan, G., *The Idea of a European Superstate: Public Justification
    and European Integration* (Princeton and Oxford: Princeton
    University Press, 2005), p.158.

10 Morgan, G., *The Idea of a European Superstate*, pp.144–146 *passim*.

11 Morgan, G., *The Idea of a European Superstate*, p.147.

12 Morgan, G., *The Idea of a European Superstate*, p.168.

13 Simms, B., 'Towards a mighty union: how to create a democratic
    European superpower', *European Ideas*, 2 April 2012.

14 O'Donnell, C.M., 'Britain's coalition government and EU defence
    cooperation: undermining British interests', *International Affairs*,
    87:2 (2011), 419–433, pp.425–433 *passim*.

15 Biscop, S., 'The UK and European defence: leading or leaving?',
    International Affairs, 6 (2012) 1297–1313, pp.1297- 1313 *passim*.

16 Worre, P., 'The consequences of a British exit from the EU and
    CDSP: An analytical timeline', *ISIS Europe and NATO Watch*,
    January 2013, p.4.

17 Vander Elst, P., *Resisting Leviathan: The Case Against a European
    State* (London: The Claridge Press, 1991), pp.25–26.

18 Hannan, D., *A Doomed Marriage: Britain and Europe* (London:
    Notting Hill Editions, 2012), pp.16–21 *passim*.

19 McDougall, W., *The Group Mind* (London: Cambridge University
    Press, 1920), pp.177–181 *passim*.

20 McDougall, W., *Ethics and Some Modern World Problems* (London:
    Methuen, 1924), pp.46–48 *passim*.

21 Kant, I., 'To Perpetual Peace: A Philosophical Sketch' (1795)
    in Kant, I., *Perpetual Peace and other essays on Politics, History
    and Morals* (Indianapolis and Cambridge: Hackett Publishing
    Company, 1983), para. 356, p.117.

22 Glendinning, S., 'A European federation of states is the only
    form of integration which has the chance to preserve freedom
    and survive shifting power relations between sovereign nations',
    Europp—European Politics and Policy Blog, 11 July 2012:
    http://blogs.lse.ac.uk/europpblog/2012/07/11/european-
    integration-kant-philosophical-triangle/

23 Glendinning, S., 'Europe should reject Jürgen Habermas' vision
    of a federal European state and instead create an enduring
    association between sovereign nations', *Europp—European Politics*

and Policy Blog, 3 September 2013:
http://blogs.lse.ac.uk/europpblog/2013/09/03/europe-should-reject-jurgen-habermas-vision-of-a-federal-european-state-and-instead-create-an-enduring-association-between-sovereign-nations/

24 Lindley-French, J., 'Why America is stuck with NATO', *Europe's World*, Autumn 2006:
http://www.europesworld.org/NewEnglish/Home_old/Article/tabid/191/ArticleType/articleview/ArticleID/20353/language/en-US/Default.aspx

25 Schmitt, O., 'A Tragic Lack of Ambition: Why EU Security Policy is no Strategy', *Contemporary Security Policy* 34, 2, 2013, 413–416, p.414.

26 Schmitt, O., 'A Tragic Lack of Ambition', p.415.

27 Coffey, L., 'Withdrawing US Forces from Europe Weakens America', *The Heritage Foundation*, 23 May 2013:
http://www.heritage.org/research/reports/2013/05/withdrawing-us-forces-from-europe-weakens-america

28 Rogers, J., 'Syria: end of the British "global era"?', *Ideas in Europe Website*, 1 September 2013:
http://europeangeostrategy.ideasoneurope.eu/2013/09/01/syria-end-of-the-british-global-era/

29 Zawahiri, A., Communique, 4 March 2006, in Mansfield, L., *His Own Words: Translation and Analysis of the Writings of Dr Ayman Al Zawahiri* (USA: TLG Publications, 2006), p.p.311–314 *passim*.

30 Whitehead, T., 'Syria a "game changer" for UK terror threat, warns Home Office intelligence chief', *Telegraph*, 3 July 2013;

31 Lindley-French, J., 'Strategic Pretence or Strategic Defence? Britain, France and the Common Security and Defence Policy after Libya', Geneva Centre for Security Policy, Policy Paper no. 14, April 2011, pp.2–3:
http://www.gcsp.ch/Regional-Capacity-Development/Publications/GCSP-Publications/Policy-Papers/Strategic-Pretence-or-Strategic-Defence-Britain-France-and-the-Common-Security-and-Defence-Policy-after-Libya

32 Gates, R.M., Speech delivered at National Defence University, Washington DC, 23 February 2010:
http://www.defense.gov/Speeches/Speech.aspx?SpeechID=1423

33 O'Donnell, C.M., 'The EU's Common Security and Defence Policy' in Centre for European Reform, *Review of the Balance of Competences between the United Kingdom and the European Union (Foreign Policy) : Submission of Evidence*, p.15:

https://www.gov.uk/government/uploads/system/uploads/
attachment_data/file/224253/evidence-centre-for-european-
reform.pdf

34 'Berlin's stance on Libya has isolated Germany in NATO',
Deutsche Welle, 13 April 2011:
http://www.dw.de/berlins-stance-on-libya-has-isolated-
germany-in-nato/a-14985036

35 Dyson, T., 'German Election Briefing – Defence Policy: An
end to the "Wasted Years"?', *Centre for European Politics Blog*, 4
September 2013:
http://cep.rhul.ac.uk/cep-blog/2013/9/4/german-election-blog-
defence-policy-an-end-to-the-wasted-yea.html

36 McNamara, S., 'Is the Special Relationship Still Special?', *Journal
of International Security Affairs*, No. 14, Spring 2008:
http://www.securityaffairs.org/issues/2008/14/mcnamara.php

37 Coffey, L., 'EU Defence Integration: Undermining NATO,
Transatlantic Relations, and Europe's Security', Heritage
Foundation, *Backgrounder* no. 2806, 6 June 2013, p.10.

38 Coffey, L., 'EU Defence Integration', p.10.

39 Rotherham, L., 'Why we should pull out of the EU Defence
Agency', *Conservative Home*, 21 May 2013:
http://www.conservativehome.com/platform/2013/05/dr-lee-
rotherham.html

40 North, R., 'Defence integration – by stealth?', *The Bruges Group*,
18 October 2004;

41 Gardiner, N., 'EU Proposals for a European Army would destroy
Nato and threaten the transatlantic alliance', 19 September 2012:
http://blogs.telegraph.co.uk/news/nilegardiner/100180784/
eu-proposals-for-a-european-army-would-destroy-nato-and-
threaten-the-transatlantic-alliance/

42 Lewis, K., 'MEPs call for suspension of EU-US SWIFT agreement
following new NSA revelations', *theparliament.com*, 10 September
2013;

43 U.S. Department of the Treasury, "Terrorist Finance Tracking
Program: Questions and Answers," [undated]:
http://www.ustreas.gov

44 Home Affairs Committee, *Pre-Lisbon Treaty EU police and criminal
justice measures: the UK's opt-in decision* (Westminster, London:
House of Commons, 2013), paras 36–37:
http://www.publications.parliament.uk/pa/cm201314/cmselect/
cmhaff/615/61504.htm
See also:

http://www.civitas.org.uk/pdf/EuropeDebateNo3Justice.pdf

45 The Rt Hon. Lord Lamont of Lerwick , 'The dangers of the EU
Arrest Warrant', *Bruges Group*, 1 May 2003:
http://www.brugesgroup.com/news.live?article=156&keyword=
10&share=1

46 Home Office, 'Evidence of Fraud and Abuse of Free Movement
in the UK', 5 February 2014:
http://europeanmemoranda.cabinetoffice.gov.uk/
files/2014/01/9124-13_Min_Cor_20_January_2014_Harper-
Cash_annex_1.pdf

47 Dufin, C. and Mendick, R., 'How we are powerless to stop the
"carousel of career beggars"', *Sunday Telegraph*, 29 September
2013.

48 Allen, P., 'Louvre closes over pickpockets', *Telegraph*, 10 April
2013

49 'David Blunkett riot fears over Roma migrant tensions', BBC
News, 12 November 2013:
http://www.bbc.co.uk/news/uk-politics-24909979?print=true

50 Raab, D., *Cooperation Not Control: The Case for Britain Retaining
Democratic Control over EU Crime and Policing Policy* (London: Open
Europe, 2012), p.42.

51 For details about all three cases and several others, see Fair Trials
International, *The European Arrest Warrant seven years on: the case
for reform* (London: Fair Trials International, 2011):
http://www.fairtrials.org/documents/FTI_Report_EAW_
May_2011.pdf

52 'Michael Turner and Jason McGoldrick guilty of Hungary fraud',
BBC News, 2 November 2012:
http://www.bbc.co.uk/news/uk-england-20543343

53 Home Office – Judicial Cooperation Unit, Transcript from the
Official Tape Recording of Evidence Session, 7 April 2011, p.2134:
https://www.gov.uk/government/uploads/system/uploads/
attachment_data/file/117545/oral-evidence-7.pdf

54 Bryant, A., *A Choice for Destiny: Commonwealth and Common Market*
(London: Collins, 1962) , pp.46–48 & *passim*.

55 Bryant, A., 'An Historian Protests', *The Director*, January 1963,
80–81; quoted in Stapleton, J., *Sir Arthur Bryant and National
History in Twentieth Century Britain* (Latham, Maryland, USA:
Lexington Books, 2005), p.261.

4: Britain's Best Way Out of the EU

1   Cameron, D., 'EU Speech at Bloomberg', 23 January 2013, *Gov.UK*:

https://www.gov.uk/government/speeches/eu-speech-at-bloomberg

2   Cameron, D., 'EU Speech at Bloomberg', 23 January 2013, *Gov.UK*
3   The main pre-referendum-pledge studies of the alternatives to Britain's EU membership are: Milne, I., *Time to Say No: Alternatives to EU Membership* (London: Civitas, 2011); Lea, R. and Brindley, B., *Britain and Europe: A new relationship* (London: Global Vision, 2012); Booth, B. and Howarth. C., *Trading Places: Is EU membership still the best option for UK trade?* (London: Open Europe, 2012); Fresh Start Project, *'Options for Change' Green Paper: Renegotiating the UK's relationship with the EU*, July 2012; and Charter, D., *Au Revoir, Europe: What if Britain left the EU?* (London: Biteback Publishing, 2012).
4   North, R., *The Norway Option: Re-joining the EEA as an alternative to membership of the European Union* (London: Bruges Group, 2013), pp.6–7:
    http://www.brugesgroup.com/TheNorwayOption.pdf
5   Hannan, D., 'Switzerland is a more attractive model than Norway, but Britain could do better than either', *Telegraph*, 15 December 2012:
    http://blogs.telegraph.co.uk/news/danielhannan/100194407/outside-the-eu-we-should-aim-to-copy-switzerland-not-norway/
6   Council conclusions on EU relations with EFTA countries, 14 December 2010; quoted in Charter, D., *Au Revoir Europe: What if Britain left the EU?* (London: Biteback Publishing, 2012), p.208.
7   Charter, D., *Au Revoir Europe*, p.210.
8   Charter, D., *Au Revoir Europe*, p.212.
9   Booth, S. and Howarth, C., *Trading Places* (London: Open Europe, 2012), p.45:
    http://www.openeurope.org.uk/Content/Documents/Pdfs/2012EUTrade.pdf
10 Chalmers, D., 'Preface' to Chapter 3 of Campbell Bannerman, D., *Time to Jump: A Positive Vision of a Britain Out of the EU and in EEA Lite* (Epsom, Surrey: Bretwalda Books, 2013), p.60.
11 Campbell Bannerman, D., *Time to Jump*, p.61.
12 Campbell Bannerman, D., *Time to Jump*, pp.61–63.
13 Campbell Bannerman, D., *Time to Jump*, p.37.
14 Campbell Bannerman, D., *Time to Jump*, pp.65–67.
15 Batten, G., 'Article 50 is a trap for the unwary', *Freedom Today*, Winter 2014, p.8.
16 'Consolidated Version of the Treaty on European Union', *Official*

Journal of the European Union, C 115/15, 9.May 2008:
http://eur-lex.europa.eu/LexUriServ/LexUriServ.do?uri=OJ:C:20
08:115:0013:0045:en:PDF

17 Milne, I., 'The EU *has* to negotiate Free Trade Agreements with
Third-Parties – and it does', *Global Britain Briefing Note*, no. 61, 7
January 2011.

18 Dixon, H., 'Brexit would be messy', *Reuters*, 21 October 2013:
http://www.reuters.com/article/2013/10/21/us-breakingviews-
britain-eu-idUSBRE99K04S20131021

19 Harris-Quinney, B., 'If you Brexit, you own it', *Bow Group*, 24
October 2013:
http://www.bowgroup.org/policy/if-you-brexit-you-own-it

20 Waterfield, B., 'Angela Merkel pushes for EU treaty change',
Telegraph, 22 October 2013:
http://www.telegraph.co.uk/news/worldnews/europe/
eu/10397512/Angela-Merkel-pushes-for-EU-treaty-change.html

21 Waterfield, B., 'Angela Merkel pushes for EU treaty change'.

22 'A Grand, Controversial Plan for Europe', *Der Spiegel*, 21 October
2013:
http://www.spiegel.de/international/germany/merkel-wants-to-
reform-eu-with-more-powers-for-brussels-a-928988-druck.html

23 Waterfield, B., 'Angela Merkel pushes for EU treaty change'.

24 'Merkel Speech: Chancellor Urges Reforms to Preserve Euro',
Spiegel Online, 18 December 2013:
http://www.spiegel.de/international/europe/merkel-calls-on-eu-
members-to-agree-binding-reforms-a-939813.html

25 Dominiczak, D., 'Merkel poised to back Cameron's push for
reform of ties with the EU', *Telegraph*, 24 February 2014:
http://www.telegraph.co.uk/news/newstopics/
eureferendum/10656991/David-Cameron-hoping-for-Merkel-
support-over-EU-negotiations.html

26 Waterfield, B., 'Angela Merkel pushes for EU treaty change'.

27 Williams, C., *Adenauer: The Father of the New Germany* (London:
Little, Brown and Company, 2000), pp.356–373 *passim*.